Altmetrics

A practical guide for librarians,
researchers and academics

Every purchase of a Facet book helps to fund CILIP's advocacy,
awareness and accreditation programmes for
information professionals.

Altmetrics
A practical guide for librarians, researchers and academics

Edited by
Andy Tattersall

facet
publishing

Published by Facet Publishing,
7 Ridgmount Street, London WC1E 7AE
www.facetpublishing.co.uk

Facet Publishing is wholly owned by CILIP: the Chartered Institute
of Library and Information Professionals.

British Library Cataloguing in Publication Data
A catalogue record for this book is available from the British
Library.

ISBN 978-1-78330-010-5 (paperback)
ISBN 978-1-78330-100-3 (hardback)
ISBN 978-1-78330-151-5 (e-book)

First published 2016

Text printed on FSC accredited material.

Typeset from editor's files by Facet Publishing Production in
10/14 pt Palatino Linotype and Myriad Pro
Printed and made in Great Britain by CPI Group (UK) Ltd,
Croydon, CR0 4YY.

Contents

Contributors

Euan Adie is founder and CEO of Altmetric.com, which supplies altmetrics data to funders, universities and publishers. Originally a computational biologist at the University of Edinburgh, in 2005 he developed postgenomic.com, which aggregated blog posts written by life scientists about published scholarly articles. This effort was supported by Nature Publishing Group, where he then worked in product management roles until starting Altmetric.com in 2011.

  Twitter: @Stew

Claire Beecroft is a university teacher/information specialist at the School of Health and Related Research (ScHARR), University of Sheffield. She currently teaches on a variety of courses within ScHARR and the wider university, including the Health Technology Assessment (HTA) MOOC (Massive Open Online Course) and the MScs in Health Informatics, Public Health and HTA. Her key research interests are around e-learning, e-health, applications of Web 2.0 to healthcare, teaching of health informatics and information skills and support for NHS librarians and staff to develop key informatics skills. Her main teaching interests are around literature searching and evidence retrieval, critical appraisal, e-health, telemedicine, media portrayal of health research and health economics, and information study skills.

  Twitter: @beakybeecroft

Dr Andrew Booth is Reader in Evidence Based Information Practice at the School of Health and Related Research (ScHARR), University of Sheffield. Between 2008 and 2014 he served as Director of Research Information (Outputs) for ScHARR, helping to prepare the School's Research Excellence Framework submission. Prior to this he worked in a wide range of roles supporting research data management, information management and evidence-based practice, and delivering writing workshops to researchers. With a background in information science, he has a particular interest in bibliometrics and literature review. He currently serves on the editorial boards of *Systematic Reviews*, *Implementation Science* and *Health Information & Libraries Journal*. Over his 33-year career to date in health information management and health services research he has authored four books and over 150 peer-reviewed journal articles.

Twitter: @andrewb77877966

Dr William Gunn is the Head of Academic Outreach for Mendeley. He attended Tulane University, New Orleans, as a Louisiana Board of Regents Fellow, receiving his PhD in Biomedical Science from the Center for Gene Therapy at Tulane University. Frustrated with the inefficiencies of the modern research process, he left academia and established the biology programme at Genalyte, a novel diagnostics start-up, then joined Mendeley. He is an Open Access advocate, co-founder of the Reproducibility Initiative and serves on the National Information Standards Organization (NISO) Altmetrics working group.

Twitter: @mrgunn

Ben Showers is a Digital Delivery Manager at the Cabinet Office, using digital technologies to transform government services and systems for the better. Previously, he worked at Jisc where he was Head of Scholarly and Library Futures, working on projects that included a shared library analytics service, as well as projects exploring the future of library systems, digital libraries, usability and digitization. He is the author of *Library Analytics and Metrics: using data to drive decisions and services* (Facet Publishing, 2015).

Twitter: @benshowers

Andy Tattersall is an information specialist at the School of Health and Related Research at the University of Sheffield, and a Mendeley Advisor for the social reference management software company. He writes and gives talks about digital academia, learning technology, scholarly communications, open research, web tools, altmetrics and social media – in particular, their application for research, teaching, learning, knowledge management and collaboration. He is very interested in how we manage information and how information overload affects our professional and personal lives. His teaching interests lie in encouraging colleagues and students to use the many tools and technologies (quite often freely) available to aid them carry out research and collaboration within the academic and clinical setting. He is Secretary for the CILIP Multimedia and Information Technology Committee.

Twitter: @Andy_Tattersall

CHAPTER 1

Introduction

Andy Tattersall

Introduction

The purpose of this chapter is to give an introduction and context to the book and its theme. It will give an overview of the changes occurring in academia right now that are part of a wider picture that includes open access, MOOCs (Massive Open Online Courses), big data, emerging learning technologies and, finally, altmetrics. It will explain why this change is happening, how it is all connected, and how some library and information professionals are at the heart of it, while others should pay heed to it. It will provide an overview of the key ideas and themes within altmetrics as well as how this fits in with existing academic cultures.

Altmetrics focuses on research artefact level metrics that are not exclusive to traditional journal papers but also extend to book chapters, posters and data sets among other items. It offers an alternative indicator of attention, review and conversation that adds a highly responsive layer to the slower to accrue traditional research metrics.

Altmetrics is one of those terms, like MOOCs and big data, that many people in academia have heard of but are not entirely sure what it means. For a start, it sounds rather geeky, and perhaps something that sits within the domain of a group of experts, for example statisticians. In reality it is much simpler than that and has a potentially much wider audience, some of whom are already unknowingly using some of the technologies that contribute to altmetrics. Altmetrics has the potential to be of use to every academic, PhD and master's student thinking of going into a research career. While the term and the concept of altmetrics have been around in popular use only since 2012, the ideas and opportunities that seek to exploit it have been around for longer.

Although altmetrics is not commonplace or widely discussed outside the offices of some fund holders, publishers, PhD students, scientists and a few librarians, it has significant traction and potential. So much so that this book was commissioned to help library and information professionals gain a better understanding of the subject. To this author's mind, librarians and information professionals have an important part to play in the use of altmetrics, and the opportunity is there for them to take, should they wish to do so.

While the altmetrics movement continues to grow and gain traction in some areas of research, it is unlikely that by the time this book is published it will be entrenched within academia. MOOCs have taken a similar length of time to appear on the radar of the university teaching community and it is likely that, for most, altmetrics is still just a blip on the horizon. There are several reasons for this, which this book will go into in detail later on.

The purpose of the book

This book sets out to achieve two things. Firstly, it is theoretical: it explains why altmetrics has come about and how it fits into the bigger picture of research and academia. Secondly, it is a practical book, as understanding the theory of altmetrics or any other new technology, platform or idea is of little value if a user cannot think of how it can be applied in the workplace. The book explains how different audiences can be reached and the methods you can employ, even with minimal resources. The contributors to this book have sought to provide you with a complete guide to the history of metrics, their importance and new developments, and to explain why some have seen the need to change how we measure and communicate scholarly outputs. The book aims to give practical advice to library and information science (LIS) professionals and academics by explaining the increasing number of tools available for researchers and librarians to measure, share, connect and communicate their research – because, while altmetrics is the reason for writing this book, it would mean very little if the connecting technologies and ideas were not also covered. To some extent altmetrics is like an iceberg; on the surface we may see only a collection of materials and measurements, while below the waterline a larger presence exists. Part of this book aims to give those supporting researchers – not only LIS professionals but also research support staff – the skills needed to deal with the many different scenarios they may come across when trying to engage research staff with new technologies. Put simply, you cannot just tell someone to try a technology in the hope that it will change how they work. Instead, you need to explain why they should change, the benefits, the pitfalls and, most importantly, the practical skills to make it happen.

On the surface, altmetrics may seem daunting to some, and doubly so to those who have not yet dipped their toes into the world of social media, networks and (to return to a much-forgotten term) Web 2.0. With so much choice available to consumers, whether it be smartphones, shoes or even bread, there can often be a problem of decision fatigue, and with altmetrics it is no different. There are literally hundreds of online and electronic tools that can now be used within the academic setting. Some, such as Twitter, are not only cross-disciplinary but also cross professional and personal boundaries. More recently an increasing number of niche and specialized academic tools have appeared, making the choice encouraging for some, and for others an even greater deterrent. These deterrents or barriers relate to issues of time, privacy, application, security and choice – the latter translating into 'why choose one technology when a better one may come along next week?'

For anyone wanting to understand altmetrics and, more importantly, to encourage others to use it, it is important to understand which tool does what and why you and academics you work with should use it. In the field of learning, technologists, lecturers and teachers apply a pedagogy to technology when they employ it, otherwise they end up using technology for the sake of it. This can be counter-productive to the learning process, as students learn how to use a technology but don't necessarily discover more about the core topic the teacher is covering. The same has to apply in research, where there is an increasing demand on academics to publish papers, win bids and prove impact, and altmetric activities may be seen as an unnecessary extra.

The research cycle

For many years now the research process and, for the most part, the researcher's environment have been stable. They can often be summarized as a simple cyclical process that begins from an idea or hypothesis, collaboration or a call by fundholders. Once researchers identify a research opportunity and obtain funds and time (although the latter is trickier to source when juggling multiple responsibilities), they begin their project in earnest and – whether it is based in the lab, the field, or a coffee house, or at their desk – at the end of the project they write up research in the hope of publishing it in some format. This is the model, and there has been little deviation from it for as long as anyone can remember. Technology may have come along to aid the process of completing the work, from word processors to high-performance computing systems, yet most other things have stayed the same. The process of promoting the published outcomes of the research was usually via a few formal, static channels, most notably the peer-reviewed journal and conference presentations. The model is still widely practised and shows little sign of changing wholesale until academics become sure of the benefits of new forms of scholarly communications.

Communication of new research has often been left for the researcher to do, whether via e-mails to personal networks or in conference presentations. Publishers have released journal 'table of contents' alerts, but in reality very little else happened beyond the research appearing on the journal shelves in the library or in searchable databases. That is, until other researchers and professional support staff ran literature searches and discovered the new-ish research. These papers then formed part of the evidence base for future research via the system of other researchers citing them.

Things have moved on somewhat since then. Journal publishers, although not employed to promote one paper over another, are doing more to disseminate research via the use of social media, while at the other end of the spectrum many researchers are taking it upon themselves to share their research and findings across the web via blogs and social media. This has of course been happening for some time in very small silos on the web, but for the most part the version 'Research 1.0', with its limited scholarly communications, is still very much the normal situation.

The course of the book

This book brings together various experts in their fields to help guide readers through the practical and technical aspects of altmetrics. Guest chapter writers help to synthesize the ideas and reasons that have led to a variety of innovations and technologies coming together with the goal of measuring research.

Chapter 2 makes the connection between altmetrics and social media and explains how we have got to where we are and where it might take us. The web, and later Web 2.0 and social media, brought about the right ingredients for the development of platforms like Mendeley, Altmetric.com and Impactstory.

Chapter 3 is written by my colleague Andrew Booth from the University of Sheffield, who is no stranger to writing for Facet Publishing on topics relating to the library and information world. Andrew provides an interesting, entertaining and concise history of traditional metrics and their development, and the reasoning and politics that have grown up alongside them.

As you will find by reading this book, altmetrics has a lot of potential not only for academics but also for fund holders, publishers and libraries. At a time when libraries are having to tighten their financial belts and cut their expenditure, altmetrics can provide some of the analytics to help tough decision making. In Chapter 4, Ben Showers, formerly of Jisc, who has previously written for Facet Publishing on analytics and metrics, covers the evolution of library metrics, including bibliometrics. Ben looks at what is happening in libraries right now and where the future seems to be pointing us to.

Euan Adie, the founder of Altmetric.com, looks at the other side of the metrics fence and altmetrics as a whole in Chapter 5. Euan's chapter, as a sequel to my Chapter 2 explaining the rise of Web 2.0 and social media, looks at the other pieces of the jigsaw and brings altmetrics firmly into the academic setting. The chapter explains the evolution of the several key players in the altmetric and academic publishing world who have tried to bring about a whole new way of looking at research outputs.

We then move on to Chapter 6, by another author well versed in altmetrics and its potential for the academic community. William Gunn is Head of Academic Outreach at Mendeley and he discusses the various ways in which Mendeley is looking at the data coming from the references that Mendeley users store in their accounts, and how this can form alternative metrics. He discusses the importance of discovering previously unseen data about published research and turning it into useful information. Previously, citations and the impact factors of journals were the means by which research was measured. William explains that these days everything from downloads, views and shares can be checked and counted and can give a new angle on academic quality. Although William is employed by Mendeley, this chapter is by no means a sales pitch for the research technology company (now owned by Elsevier), but gives a balanced view of where this arm of scholarly communication and measurement is going.

My Chapter 7 aims to give practical advice to LIS professionals and academics on how they can employ altmetrics and the associated technologies in their organizations. The chapter provides a mixture of tactics and case studies that can be used to help make the most of new ideas and technologies, especially in the face of inertia and technology-platform overload.

Chapter 8, again written by me, is about the great variety of altmetrics and related tools that can be used by LIS professionals and academics. One of the issues touched on in Chapter 7 is that of inertia and organizational change. Researchers and LIS professionals face the problem not only of technology choice but also that of understanding each technology and its application. It can be hugely time-consuming to explore new websites and technologies, especially when another, better solution can be just around the corner. The purpose of Chapter 8 is to give brief summaries of the technologies and the ideas behind them, and thus relieve LIS professionals of the job of exploring what is available. The list is by no means complete, as only a wiki or online bookmark could achieve that feat. The chapter also presents various scenarios to help readers make the connection between the technology and the use – in essence, the research pedagogy. The list is by no means exhaustive, as new tools are appearing every week and their use is subjective; one tool may be seen in an altmetric context by one person but not by another. The chapter aims to demonstrate why, in this author's opinion, each tool is worthy of note in the altmetric setting. Some tools are very niche, and others are purely transient in their use, in that you may use them only once to achieve a goal.

Chapter 9 investigates the increasingly important topic of post-publication peer review. Although it is not always associated as an altmetric and is still very new to most academics, post-publication review, anonymous or otherwise, remains a contentious topic in some domains of academia. The purpose of peer review is to measure and assess the quality of a piece of academic work. Post-publication review is the same, but happens after a paper has been published. Its output is very similar to that of altmetrics in that it gives new insights into a piece of published work. It also provides opportunities for collaboration between authors as they start to discover other researchers who are engaged with similar ideas and work.

Chapter 10 is written by Claire Beecroft, from my department at the University of Sheffield, who looks of the opportunities that can be afforded by making better use of mobile or tablet devices. Altmetric tools have yet to appear in any kind of notable numbers on mobile devices, yet this is only a matter of time. On the other hand, online tools for sharing (such as Twitter) and writing (such as blogs) can now be accessed easily. Given that this book discusses the problems of information overload and time management, it is important for LIS professionals and researchers to discover how to make better use of their smart devices as part of a seamless altmetrics experience.

The penultimate chapter is about the process of open peer review, an area that is increasingly being discussed within the academic community and has much similarity to altmetrics. Whether this process takes place before a piece of research is published, or afterwards, when a long tail of scholarly dialogue is opened up, it is, like altmetrics, a challenge to the status quo. The chapter discusses the pros and cons of open peer review and looks at some of the leading platforms, whether they be journals, databases or small third-party startups. The book concludes by reviewing the issues covered in the previous chapters and discussing whether altmetrics has a future. It aims to predict – although in technology that's a pretty tough call – whether, in time, altmetrics can gain wider appeal and traction. Since I was asked to write this book, back in 2013, a lot of things have changed. Altmetrics has shown no signs of going away, but neither has it replaced traditional metrics. I will discuss what that means for academia and whether, in my view, we will ever find an ideal solution to the problem we now face with regard to scholarly metrics and communication since the advent of the web and, more importantly, the social web.

Conclusion

Altmetrics has not happened by chance; if anything, things have been percolating for some years, thanks to a mixture of social and cloud-based academic and non-academic websites and tools. Jason Priem first used the term 'altmetrics' in a tweet back in 2010, and this was part of the driving force for Mendeley, figshare, Impactstory, Altmetric.com and others to bring disparate communities and ideas together under its banner. As someone whose role is very much to keep an ear to the ground for new ways of working and technologies, it was inevitable that I would come across altmetrics – which, according to my e-mail archive, I did in April 2012. Alongside other technologies and ideas that I have promoted and investigated, I try to maintain an objective view. It can be too easy to be swept up by new platforms and ideas and decide that everything that came before is now redundant. But constantly moving forward can have its pitfalls, as too little time may be given to reflection and gaining a deeper understanding of an idea or technology. Yet, as in the case of MOOCs for the teaching side of the academic organization, change is inevitable, thanks to technologies. While MOOCs have not destroyed or revolutionized universities on the scale that some predicted, they have driven many to assess existing systems and cultures.

Altmetrics exists, and is to some extent gaining a foothold. In various research areas, decision makers, fundholders, publishers and researchers are starting to take notice. In late 2014 the first European altmetrics residential conference took place at the Wellcome Trust in London – although one should also note that a one-day altmetrics conference had taken place in the USA two years earlier, featuring some of the key protagonists. The Wellcome hosted an inaugural altmetrics conference, quite fittingly titled 1:AM, which quickly sold out. It featured a series of workshops and discussions by fund holders, publishers, researchers, librarians and altmetricians, if such a term exists. The conference addressed many issues, notable among them being one raised by Jeremy Farrar, the Director of the Wellcome Trust, who said: 'We are in danger of overburdening the research community with ever more approaches, and it is on the edge of not being able to cope…such that we will destroy [its] creativity and innovation.'

As with MOOCs, it is possible that altmetrics may not be the end product, but a path to something else. Hopefully, that will be something sustainable and transferable that provides value to everyone and everything, but only time will tell. If altmetrics is to gain traction in research and its end result is to lead to something else that improves scholarly communication and measurement, it will have achieved its aim. In order to do this, we need a better understanding of why this is happening and how we can iron out any wrinkles. Simply burying one's head in the sand and continuing as before, when the world outside is changing, is no longer acceptable. Change can be very frightening and not always for the better; hence the need to understand what these tools can do. When an academic asks you about a tool like Twitter or Mendeley, your advice can be about more than just the technical dimension, and can also be about how these things all connect together to aid scholarly communication and measurement.

Research is being formally measured, and the word 'impact' is appearing evermore in offices and meetings across academia. Like governments and their policies, the ways in which research is measured and rewarded are changing, and will continue to change in a web-focused world. The altmetrics story still has some way to go, and how it plays out is anyone's guess. The seeds have been sown and the technology is being put to use by various individuals and organizations. This book aims to explore all of the possibilities, and to give readers a balanced view of them and whether they should be exploited by the researchers whom LIS professionals support.

CHAPTER 2

Road map: from Web 2.0 to altmetrics

Andy Tattersall

Introduction

This chapter aims to give readers a better understanding of why altmetrics and other allied social media tools have evolved that have the potential to change academia, the library and information world. The purpose is to explain that this change has not happened overnight and that it is part of a much bigger shift that is taking place. During the decade 2005–15 Web 2.0 technologies have afforded academia several opportunities, and only now are we starting to take advantage of them. Much of the academic and library community has been slow to embrace technologies focused on scholarly communication and measurement. This chapter explains the continually evolving process, and that in reality there is still some way to go before we will see academics using what we would previously have referred to as Web 2.0 tools fluently in their workflow. The chapter explains how past and present technologies have developed and been exploited in the library community. Given the ascendency of social media and Web 2.0 in academia and libraries, it was only a matter of time before alternative metrics appeared, in whatever form.

The beginning of the web

For anyone under the age of 35 it is hard to imagine life without the internet, while anyone over that age who regularly uses it will probably feel that it has been around for most of their working life. This is testament to the impact and significance of such an invention; it has changed the world beyond recognition. We cannot touch it, smell it or taste it, yet the world wide web has become an essential part of billions of people's existence. Academia has been part of the web since day one; indeed it was a computer scientist, Sir Tim Berners-Lee, who put a proposal to his employers at CERN, the European Organization for Nuclear Research, for an information management system in 1989. Within the first few years of the web's existence various notable academic websites were established. These included the pre-print archive arXiv.org in 1991 and the bioinformatics resource portal ExPASy two years later.

Academia was an early utilizer of the many technologies that came pre and post the development of the web interface to perform a multitude of tasks. These included e-mail for communication, networking for data transfer, forums for topic discussion, public-facing websites for promotion and intranets for private and sensitive information. Yet it was slow to explore the benefits of the web's younger sibling, Web 2.0, which appeared around 2004. Fifteen years after Sir Tim Berners-Lee refined and revealed to the world his own project that we came to know as the web, an iteration appeared that was quickly named Web 2.0. The term started to be popularized within certain internet communities, primarily the tech and academic ones. Originally documented by Darcy DiNucci (1999) some five years earlier, it was popularized by Dale Dougherty (O'Reilly, 2005) of O'Reilly Media. By this time O'Reilly and his associates, who had driven the popularity of the term 'open source' back in 1998, were well versed in the web.

What Web 2.0 changed

The core element of Web 2.0 was that it changed the way we interacted with the web. Instead of a one-way relationship between the web host and visitor, where users were limited to viewing web content in the form of text, images and video, they could now interact with it and create their own similar content. The web could now be manipulated by wider audiences without the need for web-authoring and publishing skills such as HTML. The new era of Web 2.0 opened up the possibility for anyone to publish, catalogue, communicate, share and network on the web, including in academia. In the decade or so since that development, little has changed in some areas of academia, which to a great extent still operates in a Web 1.0 world. E-mail remains dominant, academic websites are mostly still static and social media remains outside the comfort zone of most academics. Research still operates on a platform where it is often conducted in private and findings are published in journals and presented at conferences. There is very little sign of the long tail (Miller, 2005) that Web 2.0 brought us through the likes of Amazon book search. While it is important to note that, by its very nature, much research requires secrecy and privacy, academia has still been slow to take advantage of the merits of Web 2.0 for disseminating research post publication. There are several possible reasons for this, the first being that a change may have happened but we did not realize it. To some extent the web has always been interactive; we could post topics on discussion forums, write e-mails, follow RSS feeds and leave comments on things such as blogs. But the facility to upload content, curate news and information, and create websites and blogs without the need for HTML was not understood by the majority in academia. This was perhaps because editing on the web was something a web designer did, but also because very little support was provided and there was little evidence to show why taking your research onto the web was a good idea. For a start, where would you begin, who would be interested in it and how much time would this take? The model of academia is one where rigorous research takes place within the lab, office or workshop, or out in the field, and for the most part the dissemination happens via journals, books and conference proceedings. Web 2.0 and, later, social media began to change that. The transition from Web 1.0 to Web 2.0 happened without many from outside the computing and information worlds taking real note of it, yet the impact was widespread.

Early examples of how libraries and academia embraced Web 2.0

Web 2.0 and social media facilitate two things above anything else: empowerment and connections. Web 2.0 allows anyone connected to the internet to manipulate and interact with the web without the need for technical knowledge. Prior to 2005 most web content was created and directed by a small minority of users. Web 2.0 opened the doors for anyone to create and share content, and has connected the world in a way that was not possible before. Even so, the second wave of web technologies has not been universally embraced. Boxen (2008) noted that librarians have often been ridiculed for either hating new technology or jumping on every new program that comes their way. The idea that we all could now create web content, from video to blogs, from wikis to websites, was quickly embraced by hobbyists, artists, commerce and activists. It also opened up many opportunities for the LIS profession. Blogs (Blair and Cranston, 2006) could be used to share library news, updates and resources. Video (Kroski, 2007) assisted the delivery of library promotion and support, and tools such as Pageflakes and Netvibes (Tattersall, Beecroft and Cantrell, 2011) could be used to create bespoke library portals that were full of useful automatically populated web resources and news feeds. In a wider academic setting, Web 2.0 opened up possibilities for self-publishing, research dissemination, communication and collaboration. Associate professor Mike Wesch has created a good example of what the transition from Web 1.0 to Web 2.0 means for society. His area of research is cultural anthropology and his 2007 video *Web 2.0… The Machine is Us/ing Us* explains this paradigm shift. The video was also a platform for Wesch to showcase his own area of research and it received over 11 million views on YouTube – an early altmetric and indicator of Wesch's work, if ever there was one. A year later the two major academic social networks ResearchGate and Academia.edu made their appearance and they have since built up a combined customer base of over 34 million users (8 million on ResearchGate, 24 million on Academia.edu). Naturally, many users are on both platforms.

Library 2.0

As with Apple and its 'i' prefix, the 2.0 suffix started to transcend Web 2.0, so we had Science 2.0, Health 2.0 and Library 2.0 (Maness, 2006). Library 2.0 was the idea that libraries offered a user-centric experience, but was not accepted universally by libraries for a variety of reasons including organizational and IT resistance and inertia (Tattersall, 2011). For example, Web 2.0 platforms such as Netvibes (Tattersall, Beecroft and

Cantrell, 2011) could offer visitors niche collections of information pulled from external locations. It was automated, free, easy to set up and worked very well. About the same time the term 'mashup' became common in libraries and universities as users combined various Web 2.0 tools to create new resources. For example, an organization could go beyond just embedding a Google Map of the library's location into its website and could create a new resource for visitors by also embedding photographs of the library into the map. It was simple, effective and cheap to do, but generally was not taken advantage of by most large organizations.

The battle between open platforms and closed organizations

Web 2.0 offered much promise to libraries, academic institutions and other large organizations such as the NHS. The technology was cheap if not free, and often was an improvement on existing off-the-shelf technologies for which organizations were paying large amounts of money. Alternatives to established academic tools started to appear, such as Prezi for PowerPoint, Mendeley for EndNote and Google Docs for Microsoft Word. However, organizations such as the NHS were deeply embedded in a culture of paying for off-the-shelf packages from large technology companies, and IT departments and senior management sounded a note of caution. Many of the post-Web 2.0 start-ups were small, often very niche and did not have the power to break into the bigger markets. Even established platforms such as Google and its Chrome browser and Drive and Blogger were locked out by IT departments that were keen to maintain the status quo on platforms such as SharePoint and Internet Explorer.

In academia there is often greater freedom to choose new platforms and tools. This meant that tools such as Mendeley, Prezi, Google Apps, WordPress, RSS and Netvibes could be utilized by individuals and groups. Some of those who began to leverage Web 2.0 tools regarded the process as a state of mind or an attitude (Birdsall, 2007). Users employed these new tools fluently, in collaboration with each other, as part of an organic process. As social media started to emerge this process extended naturally, with many librarians and academics adapting to the new open platforms in new and inventive ways.

Digital natives and immigrants

The notion of digital natives and digital immigrants is increasingly becoming irrelevant, but nonetheless many of the new academic and altmetric technologies that have surfaced since 2008 have been created by early-career academics who would be described as natives. They have combined their understanding of academia and the new web, with the intention of changing how we communicate, collaborate and measure research. The changes that we are seeing, although not yet widespread, are being led by many who are starting out on their research careers. For example, Mendeley was set up by three German PhD students in London, Impactstory by a post-doc research student and a PhD student. Not all tools begin life like this; some are created by journal publishers, others by mid-career researchers. Nevertheless, there are several academic-focused tools that are the brain-children of individuals rather than of large groups. These include figshare, WriteLaTeX, The Winnower and Altmetric.com, to name but a few.

Conclusion

The interesting thing to note about social media and other forms of web technology in academia is how slowly they have taken hold. Universities were early adopters of the internet and web and in developing their own online presences. Yet, when Web 2.0 appeared they were cautious in embracing its potential. We have had social media platforms such as Twitter and Facebook since 2006 and 2004 and the specialist academic platforms Academia.edu and ResearchGate followed in 2008. Although uptake of the latter two may be in the tens of millions, many users are still unsure of their full purpose. Even a useful tool such as Twitter is used in a meaningful way by only a minority of academics. Academia's slowness to embrace the social web and Web 2.0 technologies – in comparison with their uptake by commerce and pornography – is perhaps indicative of an inward-facing world view. The view that academia operates in an ivory tower, or certainly on a silo level, is not without justification.

Yet things are changing in academia, most notably through open access, MOOCs and emphasis on the importance of demonstrating impact. These changes and others are being brought about by a more open and connected academia. Further achievements in this area will come through a greater understanding of the opportunities offered by tools that are the legacy of Web 2.0. An understanding of the issues and pitfalls of the new ways of working is also needed. At present, using social media, networks and altmetrics is not a prerequisite of a researcher's role, and it may never be. However, the early adopters of these technologies have helped to identify and iron out some of the issues of their use in a web-based academic landscape. By their very nature, researchers demand evidence of their decision-making processes. Developments like the web and e-mail were obvious additions to the academic's arsenal, but this is not so clear in the case of social media and developments such as altmetrics. The biggest issue that academics face in a post-Web 2.0 world is the sheer number of technologies and platforms. To some extent they can be forgiven for feeling bewildered by the breadth of choice. Many academics will claim to have benefitted by adopting these technologies early; others will have fallen by the wayside or had negative experiences. Those with good online presences, who have worked out how the web can be leveraged as a communication tool and who employ altmetrics as a measurement of that communication, will be in a better position than their peers. We are in a state of flux, and only time will tell whether there will be a paradigm shift in how academics work with the web and academy-specific tools.

Key points

- Academia was quick to employ the web and e-mail as forms of communication.
- It has been less successful in adapting to the changes afforded by Web 2.0 and social media.
- Early adopters of Web 2.0 and social media have benefitted from being able to network and communicate their research on a potentially global scale.

References

Birdsall, W. (2007) Web 2.0 as a Social Movement,*Webology*, **4** (2), a40, www.webology.org/2007/v4n2/a40.html.

Blair, J. and Cranston, C. (2006) Preparing for the Birth of Our Library Blog, *Computers in Libraries*, **26** (2), 10–13, http://cat.inist.fr/?aModele=afficheN&cpsidt=.

Boxen, J. L. (2008) Library 2.0: a review of the literature, *Reference Librarian*, **49** (1), 21–34, www.informaworld.com/smpp/content~db=all~content= a904277737~frm=titlelink.

DiNucci, D. (1999) Fragmented Future, *Print*, **4** (July/August), 32–4.

Kroski, E. (2007) The Social Tools of Web 2.0: opportunities for academic libraries, *Choice*, **44** (12), 2011–21, http://eprints.rclis.org/3852/.

Maness, J. M. (2006) Library 2.0 Theory: Web 2.0 and its implications for libraries, *Webology*, **3** (2), www.webology.org/2006/v3n2/a25.html.

Miller, P. (2005) Web 2.0: building the new library, *Ariadne*, www.ariadne.ac.uk/issue45/miller.

O'Reilly, T. (2005) *Web 2.0*, www.ttivanguard.com/ttivanguard_cfmfiles/pdf/dc05/dc05session4003.pdf.

Tattersall, A. (2011) How the Web Was Won . . . by Some, *Health Information and Libraries Journal*, **28** (3), 226–9, www.ncbi.nlm.nih.gov/pubmed/21831222.

Tattersall, A., Beecroft, C. and Cantrell, A. (2011) Using Web 2.0 Tools to Create Customized Research Portals, *Journal of Electronic Resources in Medical Libraries*, **8** (4), 367–81, www.tandfonline.com/doi/abs/10.1080/15424065.2011.626346.

Web resources

Library 2.0 – The Future of Libraries in the Digital Age: www.library20.com/.

Mike Wesch, Web 2.0 … The Machine is Us/ing Us: https://www.youtube.com/watch?v=6gmP4nk0EOE.

Further reading

Bradley, P. (2015) *Social Media for Creative Libraries*, Facet Publishing.

O'Reilly, T. (2009) *What is Web 2.0: design patterns and business models for the next generation of software* (e-book), Sebastopol, CA, O'Reilly Media.

Rogers, E. M. (2003) *Diffusion of Innovations*, 5th edn, Free Press,

Shorley, D. and Jubb, M. (eds) (2013) *The Future of Scholarly Communication*,

Facet Publishing.

Swanson, T. A. (2012) *Managing Social Media in Libraries: finding collaboration, coordination and focus*, Chandos Publishing.

CHAPTER 3

'Metrics of the trade': where have we come from?

Andrew Booth

Introduction

Paradoxically, with altmetrics in the ascendancy, the scholarly world is witnessing a renaissance of interest in traditional metrics. This chapter examines long-standing and recent drivers for metrics from the complementary perspectives of scientists, research organizations and funding agencies. It outlines established metrics for individuals (e.g. citations and the h index) and for teams and journals (the journal impact factor and other proprietorial alternatives). It examines the extent to which these metrics correlate to other important characteristics such as newsworthiness and journal prestige. The h index is an author-level metric which scores academics by their most cited papers. For example, if an academic has ten papers that are each cited ten times, their h index is 10. If they have ten papers cited no more than once each, their h index is 1.

The chapter considers challenges raised by the emerging 'impact agenda', including a need to capture 'impact on society, social impact, real-world impact, knowledge translation, and uptake by the public' (Eysenbach, 2011). It also describes how both traditional and impact metrics have been used in a variety of research and performance management contexts, giving examples of appropriate and inappropriate use.

The chapter examines criticisms of established measures and how these criticisms might, at least in theory, be addressed. It discusses manipulation and game playing which exploit acknowledged weaknesses of metrics, and provides high-profile examples. It examines the extent to which relatively recent forms of publishing, such as open access journals, are accommodated by, or pose challenges to, traditional metrics.

The chapter sets the scene for the considered evaluation of altmetrics that follows in subsequent chapters. It concludes by examining whether traditional metrics still occupy a role within a world that is increasingly populated by social media and social networks.

On metrics and madness

In Prokofiev's *Lieutenant Kijé*, a slip of a clerk's pen on a list of officers for promotion compiled for a mad tsar leads to the creation of the fictitious hero. Fearful of displeasing the mad tsar, his advisers manufacture increasingly elaborate escapades for the imaginary Kijé, each one rewarded by a successive promotion. Finally, following Kijé's promotion to general, the tsar wants to meet the hero whose career he has followed with interest. His alarmed courtiers 'kill off' the tsar's protégé and manufacture the death and funeral of the now General Kijé. In 1986, in an instance of life imitating art, de Lacey, Record and Wade (1985) revived an account from the 1930s (Dobell, 1938) of a classic error of this type. The title of a paper published in a Czechoslovakian medical journal in 1887 began 'O uplavici', the Czech (Bohemian) phrase for 'On dysentery'. In error, this phrase was transcribed as the author's name, Uplavici O, by an abstracter. Like Kijé, the fictional O Uplavici enjoyed prodigious longevity, surviving for some 50 years and even acquiring a doctorate from an American indexer in 1910!

Like the mad tsar in Prokofiev's opus, the academic community continues to attach unwarranted significance to the metrics of its printed outputs. Many promotions are attributable to the interpretation or, indeed, misinterpretation of such metrics, and no doubt this is equally true of the occasional doctorate. A Carnegie Foundation study (Boyer, 1990) reported that universities in the USA typically count citations or publications when reviewing their faculty for tenure, promotions, demotions, merit increases, etc. While the time for 'killing off' traditional metrics lies in the unspecified future, this chapter seeks to document the past and present of established academic metrics.[1] In doing so, we hope to inform the ongoing critical use of an emerging battery of altmetrics.

Drivers for metrics

For centuries, peer review has been the vehicle for determining qualitatively whether research is appropriate, represents good value for money and can make a useful contribution to society (Reedijk, 1998). However, as van Raan (2003) observes: 'Opinions of experts may be influenced by subjective elements, narrow-mindedness and limited cognitive horizons.' Bibliometrics is seen as one way of addressing such limitations, but van Raan demonstrates that this may simply exchange one set of imperfect judgements for another. The creation of the Science Citation Index in 1961 was the catalyst for the emergence of citation analysis as an independent field of study (MacRoberts and MacRoberts, 1989). Initially the Institute of Scientific Information (ISI) was very proprietorial about its innovative ranking systems. In recent years alternatives have included the Scopus system, preferred by the UK Research Excellence Framework, and Google Scholar, which, because of its broader, 'more democratic' reach, typically demonstrates higher citation counts and more incorrect citations (Harzing and van der Wal, 2008).

Numerous drivers underpin the relentless move towards scientometrics, including bibliometrics. From a political perspective there is increased pressure for judicious use of public monies as universities and research centres seek to demonstrate scientific performance and wider societal impact. Use of seemingly objective measures gives the public a more transparent picture of scholarly activity. Economically the knowledge economy requires research to offer return on investment. Metrics also fuel competition among academics, allegedly with a positive effect on scientific quality and productivity. Socially, universities and other academic institutions seek to provide evidence that they are making an 'impact', particularly in bringing research findings to bear on pervasive societal problems. Technologically, the publication chain is easier to monitor and measure, from early sharing of protocols and proposals through to submission of the archaically titled 'manuscript', its subsequent dissemination and the resultant social network activity. Underpinning the above is a belief in the collective wisdom of crowds, with the implication that the judgements of an academic community are less subjective than those of the individual researcher themselves.

Amateur bibliometrics

Van Raan (2005) appropriately characterizes the use of citation and publication counts in determining academic progression as 'amateur bibliometrics'. This counting culture is predicated on the belief that bibliometric techniques can somehow measure the 'otherwise elusive concepts of quality and influence' (Schoonbaert and Roelants, 1996). Objections to this assumption lie in how such metrics are calculated and, more significantly, in how they are misinterpreted and misapplied. Three brief and diverse examples illustrate such limitations. The impact factor, an established and manufactured metric, relates the number of citations to the number of citable articles within a two-year period. Why two years? Many studies take more than two years to make their academic mark. Indeed in the pre-web era it would take more than two years to discover that a paper existed, let alone to publish a paper that cited it. Is a journal's reputation to be assessed within such a transitory evaluation period?

The h index, a metric that seeks to capture both the quality and quantity of academic outputs, states that an author has index h if h of his or her total number of papers have at least h citations each and the remaining papers have $\leq h$ citations each. Therefore an h index of 26 indicates that 26 papers by that author have each been cited 26 or more times (Hirsch, 2005).

In another example, the h index is calculated from any authorial contribution, regardless of the author's position in the author order. A lead author with a handful of publications, each cited hundreds of times, could acquire an h index inferior to that for a research assistant who has contributed to 20 or more modestly cited publications as seventh author. Finally, numbers of citations vary significantly by discipline, regardless of how problematically 'discipline' is defined. The relative performance of the same article differs according to whether its authors decide to publish it in a journal of its own or another discipline, or in a generalist journal, such as the *British Medical Journal* in medicine. Furthermore, the number of citations is affected by such extrinsic considerations as editorial policies regarding open access, the publishing house to which a journal is affiliated, and even whether the chosen journal is included in a bundle of journals offered as a discount package to university libraries. Before we judge such flawed metrics too harshly we must recall that prior to the development of recent methods of research assessment, research funds were allocated according to raw numbers of students. We can at least celebrate the fact that the current regime no longer perpetuates 'big is beautiful' in such an overt way, although undoubtedly this mantra still exercises a covert influence.

The above examples reflect that traditional metrics operate at one of three levels:

1 in assessing individual performance
2 in evaluating the performance of a research team, group, department or institution
3 in recognizing the contribution of a journal.

A further dimension to mention in passing is whether metrics are designed to measure the performance of the researcher or of the research. We will now look at the above three levels in turn.

Assessing individual performance

Although individual academic performance is frequently measured through such measures as the number of articles published, the number of PhD students supervised, the value of research awards – particularly as principal investigator – not to mention one's h index or the number of citations to individual articles, the strength of these metrics derives from their multiplicity, not their specificity. The value attributed to each individual metric may vary according to the priorities of a particular institution, or even the time period within which particular targets are set. Metrics such as the h index are not sensitive to the current time period – they are uni-directional and only increase, never decrease. Within health services research an h index increases by one point for every year that an individual has operated as a full-time researcher. The h index is frequently disassociated with recent achievement or performance.

Other metrics carry intrinsic assumptions and thus favour particular models of research – for example, the role of the principal investigator is clearly different in a culture of small, specialist research teams when compared with large, multidisciplinary research teams where each co-investigator makes an idiosyncratic and valued contribution. Different disciplines observe different conventions in relation to the ordering of author names within an article, with differing interpretations placed on the last-named author. Authorial positioning may variously reflect advancing alphabetical order, diminishing contribution or a political statement of research leadership – sometimes conflating the latter two factors! Medicine is witnessing a move to acknowledge the extent of the contribution, to specifying the exact nature of that contribution and to attributing most value to the first-named author and to the author corresponding with the journal editor. Clearly, traditional metrics differentiate poorly between different assumptions within differing research cultures, making the use of common metrics within the same university or their transferability across institutions persistently problematic.

Evaluating the performance of a research team, group, department or institution

The use of bibliometric measures to evaluate the performance of a research team or institution typically represents an imperfect and inadequate attempt to turn a very general indicator of performance into a specific performance indicator (PI) (Bence and Oppenheim, 2005). In fact, commentators make a useful distinction whereby PIs, unlike a simple indicator (such as an objective numerical figure), 'imply a point of reference . . . or comparator, and are therefore relative rather than absolute' (Bence and Oppenheim, 2005). Experience from traditional metrics suggests that we need a more nuanced understanding of what is indicated by a particular performance measure if it is to be used in other than a crude and misleading way. To illustrate with the performance of two fictional research groups, Team Alpha and Team Numeric; Team Alpha employs a traditional 'best appropriate choice' to selection of journals for its published outputs. If rejected by its first-choice journal it goes for the next appropriate journal, and so on. In contrast, Team Numeric selects initial target journals on the basis of their impact factor and, all things being equal, other efficiency considerations such as journal rejection rate and average time to publication. At the end of year five the performance of Team Numeric, unsurprisingly, outstrips that of its Team Alpha rival when evaluated simply in terms of citations and impact factors. Does this mean that Team Numeric is the better-quality research team? In actuality we face three responses to this questionable verdict: (1) taking the indicator at face value, we reward

Team Numeric for its game playing; (2) we discredit any assessments based on such a manipulable indicator, dismissing the metrics as 'immature'; or (3) we mitigate the impact of this single measure, surrounding it with other metrics with similar inadequacies. Use of a battery of measures does not necessarily make a valid verdict more likely. Multiple measures may simply make it more problematic and time consuming to identify a single game-playing strategy!

Recognizing the contribution of a journal

When authors choose the journal in which to publish they typically effect a compromise between aspiration and expectation. Generally, an author seeks to publish in a journal with as high an impact factor as possible. However, additional considerations include the journal's particular niche, how the journal is viewed by a 'college' of similar authors, the likelihood of rejection and the amount of time the author expends on 'salvage' strategies, if rejected. A journal's rejection rate may superficially appear as an informative measure of journal quality – to re-interpret Groucho Marx's quip about not wanting to 'belong to any club that will accept people like me as a member' – yet it is clearly an independent measure of supply, both within a particular discipline and to a particular editorial office. Furthermore, there is a profound difference between acceptance for a print journal, which is partly determined by predetermined page budgets and subscription rates, and for an open access electronic journal, where editorial office capacity emerges as critical, given the comparatively negligible cost of additional electronic pages, supplements or online appendices. Qualitative assessments of a journal's quality may relate to its longevity, the calibre of its editorial board, the reputation of its publisher, affiliation to a scientific organization and the list goes on. More controversially, judgements may depend on where the journal hosts its editorial office and the pedigree of other journals in the publisher's stable. Clearly it is problematic to determine an unambiguous cause and effect between such qualitative factors and the perceived 'academic quality' of the journal title. It is even more challenging to relate a single metric, such as the journal impact factor, as unequivocally reflecting quality. Correspondence in *Nature* (Dimitrov, Kaveri and Bayry, 2010) describes how the journal *Acta Crystallographica Section A* experienced a meteoric increase in impact factor from 2.051 in 2008 to 49.926 in 2009, to leapfrog *Nature* (31.434) and *Science* (28.103) (Grant, 2010). Close analysis revealed that the article 'A short history of SHELX' included the sentence: 'This paper could serve as a general literature citation when one or more of the open-source SHELX programs . . . are employed in the course of a crystal-structure determination.' As a consequence, the article received more than 6600 citations. This article became an incredible outlier in a journal where each article is cited on average three times; the second-most-cited article in the same journal in the same year had only 28 citations. Of course the scale of this prodigious citation rate will attract further citations! Has the journal become 25 times better by accepting a single manuscript?

Table 3.1 illustrates different types of existing metrics that are captured by systems or by reputation and profile.

Table 3.1 *Different categories of metrics captured by systems or by reputation and profile*

Category of performance	Illustrative 'metric'
Popularity	Number of citations
Newsworthiness	Number of mentions in the media; column inches
Reputation	Number of research grants Value of research
Profile	Number of registered PhD students
Research supervision and management	Number/percentage of completing PhD students (within specified time period) Average time to completion for PhD students
Accessibility and popularity	Journal impact factor Normalized citation rates
Quantity/quality	h index
Impact (reach and significance)	Impact case study

Relationship to quality

We acknowledge that, *overall and on average*, there is a relationship between traditional metrics and the likely quality of published outputs. Highly cited articles do tend to appear in high-impact journals which do tend to attract the best research from the most distinguished authors. A large analysis of citations to articles in emergency medicine revealed that the citation count of articles was partly predicted by the impact factor of the journal in which they appeared and, to a more limited extent, by the quality of the articles (Callaham, Wears and Weber, 2002). However, there are important reservations to this statement. First, traditional metrics lack sensitivity to additional factors relating to academic quality. Conversely, they may attach inappropriate value to factors at best irrelevant or, more alarmingly, subject to systematic error or bias. Thus a study examining citations to papers reporting randomized trials in hepato-biliary disease found a significant association with a positive outcome. However, the study found no association of numbers of citations with adjudged quality (Kjærgard and Gluud, 2002).

Broadening the picture, four different studies on levels of evidence in medical and/or psychological research emphasize the apparent inconsistency of results. Two studies of surgery journals found a correlation between impact factor and position within the hierarchy of evidence (Obremskey et al., 2005; Lau and Samman, 2007). However, a contemporaneous study of anaesthesia journals failed to find any statistically significant correlation between journal rank and evidence-based medicine principles (Bain and Myles, 2005). The variation encountered among scientific journals is further revealed by a study of seven medical/psychological journals which found highly varying adherence to statistical guidelines, irrespective of journal rank (Tressoldi et al., 2013). Analysis of statistical power in neuroscience studies (Button et al., 2013) found no significant correlation between statistical power and journal rank. The overall pattern from these studies suggests that journal rank is a poor proxy for methodological quality.

Colquhoun (2003) recounts his experience from publishing in *Nature* (with a then impact factor of 27.9) and being cited only 57 times, while another work published in a much lower-impact journal (3.1) attained more than 400 citations! Clearly, publication in a high-impact journal does not guarantee that a paper will achieve the 'much-desired dream of the author: to be read, cited, and remembered' (Albuquerque, 2010). In our own example, the main report of a two-year project, published within a monograph series with an impact factor of over 4.0, received only 18 citations, whereas a methodological paper in a journal with an impact factor of only 2.37, a by-product of team musings during the main project, enjoyed 264 citations in the same time interval.

Traditional metrics conflate factors that are conceptually different, for example the popularity of an article and its intellectual contribution. This is analogous to ranking the performance of a sports team by the average number of spectators that view the team's matches. Although some studies demonstrate an association between quality and number of citations, a significant number of studies fail to confirm this association. West and McIlwaine (2002) examined the association of peer ratings of quality and numbers of citations between 1997 and 2000 to articles appearing in the journal *Addiction* in 1997. Although two independent reviewers agreed moderately in their ratings of the papers, the correlation between these ratings and the number of citations was almost zero. More alarmingly, one factor that was correlated with citation count was the region of origin of the first author of the paper. Noticeably, papers from English-speaking countries received more citations than those from continental Europe. These in turn received more than papers from the rest of the world. The reader will note that subjective evaluation of papers, using a range of unspecified cues, is here being used as a comparator to objective evaluation. The two raters may be consistently 'wrong' or, more likely, their shared perception of quality relates to intrinsic qualities that are imperfectly captured by more objective measures. This study illustrates the associated challenges of measuring quality and of devising a methodology by which to demonstrate such associations.

Why people cite

Key to the confusion surrounding the use of metrics is the variety of reasons why people cite other authors. The worst offence an academic can perpetuate against a fellow academic is not to misquote or wrongly cite them but to ignore their work completely! Not only do numerous motives (psychological, sociological, political, historical etc.) influence an author's decision to cite a study, but the relative influence of these motives is likely to vary from discipline to discipline. Co-citation, rather than measuring scientific quality, may in fact more accurately document the existence of a common paradigm and/or a community of interest (Simkin and Roychowdhury, 2003).

Further complexity derives from the finding that many authors categorically do not read the papers they cite from (Simkin and

Roychowdhury, 2003). Simkin and Roychowdhury estimate that only 20% of authors have read the work they cite. It is unclear whether this statistic will improve with greater open access to citable sources or whether, conversely, it will get worse as it becomes easier to identify relevant work through internet search engines and social bookmarking.

Criticisms of established metrics

Numerous criticisms of the impact factor reveal that it falls short of established requirements for validity. For example, the impact factor is not completely transparent or consistently reproducible (Rossner, Van Epps and Hill, 2007). It is potentially manipulable. However, many criticisms stem not from questionable validity but more from inappropriate use (EASE, 2007).

Inappropriate use of the impact factor includes comparison across disciplines. Citation rates, distributions and patterns are highly diverse. Such variation can be detected across broad categories, for example when comparing mathematical sciences with biological sciences. However, significant variation may pertain within disciplines, as when comparing medicine with dentistry, nursing or public health. Some degree of subject normalization is required. Nonetheless, deciding the boundaries for the field to be normalized is logistically and conceptually challenging.

Mathematically, the assumptions underlying the impact factor are equally open to debate. Put simply, the impact factor is an arithmetic mean. Statistics 101 affirms that an arithmetic mean is inappropriate as a metric for data with a skewed distribution (Joint Committee, 2008). To illustrate, about 90% of *Nature*'s 2004 impact factor was based on only a quarter of its publications. Should we be attributing a metric to a journal where about three-quarters of its publications perform worse than 'average' (Nature, 2005)?

Technically, concern has been expressed, with the advent of digital publications, that the 'purity' of the impact factor as a measure has been diluted by so many confounding factors (digital only, digital and print, early view, payment for 'gold access', etc.) (Lozano, Larivière and Gingras, 2012). The potential for manipulation is further increased by the fact that digital journals without a print equivalent are not bounded by restrictions on the number of articles that they can accept.

When journal prestige is the battleground, such concerns are significant enough. However, debates regarding appropriateness are further intensified when the impact factor is proposed as a measure by which to evaluate institutional performance, as has been the case within the UK. Reworking the debate to assessment of the quality of individual articles, not the reputation of the journal in which they are published, has alleviated concerns. However, given the short time-span within which panel assessors assign each verdict, suspicion remains regarding the influence of a journal's impact factor as a proxy for article quality.

Notwithstanding ongoing misgivings regarding the inappropriate use of impact factors as a single metric for journal or article excellence, progress has been made. More assessors are acknowledging that the impact factor should definitely not be used to assess individual researchers or institutions (Seglen, 1997; EASE, 2007). This emerging consensus is concisely summarized in the EASE Statement (2007), which recommends that 'journal impact factors are used only – and cautiously – for measuring and comparing the influence of entire journals, but not for the assessment of single papers, and certainly not for the assessment of researchers or research programmes'. Logically, such caution extends to other bibliometric measures examined at an individual level. The German Research Foundation (DFG) has published guidelines to evaluate only articles and not bibliometric information on candidates in all decisions concerning 'performance-based funding allocations, postdoctoral qualifications, appointments, or reviewing funding proposals, [where] increasing importance has been given to numerical indicators such as the h-index and the impact factor' (DFG Press Release, 2010). Other influential bodies such as the National Science Foundation (USA) and the Research Assessment Exercise (UK) have taken a similar stance.

In the UK, a move parallel to renewed interest in bibliometric measures has seen the opening up of the 'impact agenda'. This movement mirrors a utilitarian focus on the usefulness of research to society – a philosophical stance guaranteed to alienate those pre-occupied with pure science, along with many within the arts and humanities research communities. Interestingly, media impact – i.e. 'newsworthiness' – is excluded from a prodigious list of evidence sources for impact. Methodologically, this recognizes that news-worthiness is particularly vulnerable to manipulation by the author and institution. Newsworthiness also encapsulates the subjective judgements of editors and editorial staff on what interests a journalist audience (Chapman, Nguyen and White, 2007). This stance may extend to the future treatment of altmetric phenomena such as Twitter, particularly given that a researcher needs to spend less time and money in stimulating interest by tweeting details of their research as compared to traditional routes such as crafting a press release. However, newsworthiness clearly contributes to numbers of citations and so cannot be entirely removed from the picture.

Manipulation and game playing
How individuals could manipulate metrics

Much alarm has been expressed at the prevalence of self-citation and its impact on citation metrics. While gratuitous self-citation is rightly condemned, as with all unashamed self-publicity, a researcher specializing in a narrow field frequently has legitimate cause to cite their own contributions. Similarly, although citation clubs or networks ('you cite my paper and I'll cite yours') are open to abuse, what is more appropriate than a group of related researchers, who form a 'virtual college', citing each other's relevant work? Arguably, researchers perform a valuable educational service by drawing a reader's attention to associated papers in the field. Indeed, the reverse argument, i.e. that in neglecting to cite relevant papers an author might be scientifically negligent, now holds increasing weight, particularly in the context of systematic reviews and the prevention of scientific waste (i.e. the commissioning of duplicate and redundant studies or the invisibility of research that is consequently underutilized in practice).

All disciplines can identify types of articles that may be widely cited, although not necessarily widely read. Basic laboratory methods, methodology texts, seminal reports of methods and publication standards are all potential candidates. For example the CONSORT statement for reporting randomized controlled trials, synchronously published in 2001 in several key journals, has attracted Google Scholar citations of over 2300 (twice – in *BMC Medical Research Methodology* and *Annals of Internal Medicine*), 2800 (*The Lancet*) and 2500 (*British Medical Journal*) in its top four publishing channels. In this unique natural experiment the open access journal *BMC Medical Research Methodology* matched *The Lancet* even though it was only in its first year of publication.

How research teams/institutions could manipulate metrics

Many routes for individual manipulation are equally open to manipulation by research teams. While co-ordinated team self-citation may increase the scale of abuse it may also increase the likelihood of detection and censure. The same mechanisms of peer review and esteem that traditionally protect the academic citadel also defend against wide-scale abuse and manipulation of traditional metrics. Instances of academic fraud and large-scale plagiarism are most frequently unearthed by fellow scientists. By implication, serendipitous discovery of citation manipulation is more likely than systematic identification of abuse. Manipulation of citations within a large research group or institution requires the determined collusion of a few influential individuals or the widespread complicity of a larger team. Nevertheless the rewards from academia, in terms of securing grants and tenure, are such that the traditional mechanisms may not be sufficient to deter systematic abuse.

How journals could manipulate metrics

While many express misgivings about the potential for manipulation and game playing, or indeed its prevalence, identified instances take the form of experiments to explore 'what if' scenarios. So, for example, the specialist journal *Folia Phoniatrica et Logopaedica* sought to demonstrate the vulnerability of the journal impact factor by publishing editorial content in 2007 that cited every single published article from that same journal over the previous two years (Opatrný, 2008). As a consequence the journal's impact factor increased from 0.66 to 1.44 until ISI suspended that journal's rating. More recently there are reported instances of 'citation stacking', i.e. collusion of journals in citing each other, with over 20 journals being suspended from ISI ratings either for this practice or for uncontrolled self-citation.

A journal can adopt editorial policies to increase its impact factor

(Monastersky, 2005; Arnold and Fowler, 2011). For example, journals may publish a larger percentage of review articles, which generally are cited more than research reports (Garfield, 1994). Thus review articles raise the impact factor of the journal and review journals often have the highest impact factors in their respective fields (Moustafa, 2014). Some journal editors set their submissions policy to 'by invitation only' so as to invite senior scientists to publish 'citable' papers in order to increase the journal's impact factor (Moustafa, 2014).

Journals may attempt to limit the number of 'citable items' – i.e. the denominator of the impact factor equation – by declining to publish articles (e.g. case reports in medical journals) that are unlikely to be cited or by altering articles (by not allowing an abstract or bibliography) in the hope that Thomson Scientific will not deem it a 'citable item'. As a result of negotiations over whether items are 'citable', impact factor variations of more than 300% have been observed (PLoS Medicine Editors, 2006). Interestingly, items considered uncitable – and thus not incorporated in impact factor calculations – can, if cited, still enter the numerator part of the equation, despite the ease with which such citations could be excluded. This effect is difficult to evaluate, as the distinction between editorial comment and short original articles is not always obvious. For example, letters to the editor may refer to either class.

Strategically, a journal might publish a large portion of its papers, or at least those expected to be highly cited, early in the calendar year. This gives papers the maximum time to gather citations. Several methods, not necessarily with nefarious intent, exist for a journal to cite articles in the same journal, which will increase the journal's impact factor (Fassoulaki et al., 2002; Agrawal, 2005).

Coercive citation is a practice in which an editor forces an author to add citations to other articles from the same journal to an article before agreeing to publish it, thereby inflating the journal's impact factor. A survey published in 2012 indicates that coercive citation has been experienced by one in five researchers working in economics, sociology, psychology and business disciplines, and it is more common in journals with a lower impact factor (Wilhite and Fong, 2012). Coercive citation has occasionally been reported for other scientific disciplines (Smith, 1997). Coercive citation is approaching extortion and is perceived by many as a violation of scientific ethics.

While these examples occupy a whole spectrum of academic practice from legitimate exploitation of the rules through to questionable conduct and malpractice, they collectively serve to illustrate the acknowledged weaknesses of existing metrics.

What have we learnt?
Assessing individual performance

Within the academic community there is growing recognition that traditional metrics must be used with caution when assessing individual performance. As Sahel (2011) observes:

> Evaluating individual research performance is a complex task that ideally examines productivity, scientific impact, and research quality – a task that metrics alone have been unable to achieve.

At the same time the author acknowledges that evaluating individual scientific performance is an essential component of research assessment. Existing measures such as impact factor, numbers of citations and the 'new indicators' (such as the h index and the g index) are all found wanting for such a task. As with the h index, the g index also provides author level metrics but these are ranked in decreasing order of the number of citations they have received. It is relatively straightforward to examine the impact factor of the journals in which a particular person has published articles. This use is widespread, but controversial. Garfield (1998) warns of the 'misuse in evaluating individuals' because there is 'a wide variation from article to article within a single journal'.

We do not conclude that more sophisticated indicators are required so as to overcome long-acknowledged deficiencies such as the inability to discriminate between author order and the prevalence of cultural and language citation patterns. Instead we endorse a more encompassing range of indicators that factor in 'teaching, mentoring, participation in collective tasks, and collaboration-building. In addition to quantitative parameters that are not measured by bibliometrics, such as number of patents, speaker invitations, international contracts, distinctions, and technology transfers' (Sahel, 2011). Clearly, the potential of altmetrics comes not so much in improving the robustness of domains measured by traditional metrics but, more cogently, in expanding the range of activities catered for when assessing academic research performance.

Evaluating the performance of a research team, group, department or institution

An inherent attraction of bibliometrics in evaluating team or institutional performance is the apparent ease and speed with which assessments are performed, particularly when compared with qualitative assessment by experts (Sahel, 2011). Haeffner-Cavaillon and Graillot-Gak (2009) describe their experience when evaluating the team performance of 600 research teams within the French research institution INSERM. They confirm that 'analysis of bibliometric indicators cannot depend on one bibliometric indicator alone but must take into account several indicators to allow having an overall picture of the team output'. They conclude that each indicator has its advantages and limitations, and that caution is required in not considering any single metric as an 'absolute' index of scientific quality. They advocate a model of 'enrichment', i.e. that metrics should inform, yet not determine, a scientific committee's debates. Furthermore, they observe that, despite the acknowledged limitations of peer review, most scientists appear to believe that such a qualitative assessment is 'the best system and agree that it is the only way to evaluate researchers'. Clearly, qualitative assessment, informed but not determined by bibliometric indicators and supplemented by a wide range of altmetrics, will persist for some considerable time as the preferred method of assessment of team or institutional performance.

Recognizing the contribution of a journal

Systems employing journal rank have been criticized for being 'not only technically obsolete, but also counter-productive and a potential threat to the scientific endeavour' (Brembs, Button and Munafò, 2013). Generally, with notable exceptions, the impact factor has achieved widespread acceptance as an indicator of overall journal quality. However, this may be associated less with overall validity and more with its ubiquitous and highly visible presence. Debates about the appropriateness of the impact factor centre on the optimal unit for comparison. Comparisons at discipline, sub-discipline or topic level attract expressions of dissatisfaction, most typically from those who feel disadvantaged within a particular constituency or configuration. Academics recognize that the distribution of numbers of citations for articles within a journal is heavily skewed, with a small number of articles holding undue influence over the overall impact factor. Impact factors may preserve the status quo, with a minimum of two years before a journal may apply for an impact factor. Under such circumstances it may be challenging to lure manuscripts away from established journals within a self-preserving hierarchy. Interestingly, the role of the impact factor has evolved to be far more about signifying the prestige of the journal targeted by a paper pre-publication (i.e. the aspiration to publish in a journal with a high impact factor). Once a paper is published, the influence of the impact-factor metric may be diluted by additional insights from individual article-level metrics.

Methodologically, the inability of the impact factor to distinguish open access journals from traditional, subscription-based journals is a current cause for concern. However, this may represent nothing more than a transitory blip in a relentless stampede towards open access. Harnad (2008) identifies collective contributors to 'Open Access Impact Advantage'. These include:

- an *early access advantage* (with a pre-print being accessible before the published post-print)
- a *quality bias* (higher-quality articles are more likely to be made open access)
- a *quality advantage* (higher-quality articles benefit more from being made open access for users who cannot otherwise afford access)
- a *usage advantage* (open access articles are more accessible, more quickly and easily, for downloading)
- a *competitive advantage* (which will vanish once all articles are open access).

He concludes that open access possesses net benefits for research and researchers across all disciplines.

A persisting challenge posed to altmetrics is the mixed economy within which journals continue to operate. At present, activity by significant numbers of paper-based readers is not factored into electronic metrics. While underreporting is one consideration, of greater concern is the non-representative distribution of readers. For example, those in developing countries may read articles in paper form and may encounter delays in receiving printed journals. However, the economics of paper journals may challenge these stereotypes as publishers recognize that offering nominally priced access to readers from developing countries, with comparatively minimal investment in additional infrastructure, may extend the potential readership and result in a net financial gain.

Some alternative traditional metrics
Related indices

Alternative traditional indices include:

- *immediacy index*: the number of citations the articles in a journal receive in a given year, divided by the number of articles published
- *cited half-life*: the median age of the articles cited in *Journal Citation Reports* each year; for example, if a journal's half-life in 2005 is 5, citations from 2001 to 2005 constitute half of all the citations from that journal in 2005, with the remaining citations preceding 2001
- *aggregate impact factor* for a subject category: calculated taking into account the number of citations to all journals in the subject category and the number of articles from all journals in the subject category
- *source normalized impact per paper (SNIP)*: a factor released in 2012 by Elsevier to estimate impact (Elsevier, 2014). The measure is calculated as SNIP=RIP/(R/M), where RIP=raw impact per paper, R = citation potential and M = median database citation potential (Moed, 2010).

These measures apply only to journals, not individual articles or individual scientists, unlike the h index. The relative number of citations that an individual article receives is better viewed as citation impact.

A note about altmetrics

While others in this book will offer expert evaluations of the future role of altmetrics, I choose to showcase the 'trad-alt paradox'. Alternative metrics (altmetrics) typically measures impact at article level. It includes article views, downloads or mentions in social media, e.g. Twitter. As a leading player in developing an online journal 'presence', the *British Medical Journal* published the number of views for its articles. These corresponded somewhat to patterns exhibited by citations (Delamothe and Smith, 2004). The paradox is this: if trad-metrics are widely considered as being flawed and of questionable accuracy, then any such correlation should, in theory, be a cause for concern, not celebration. Additionally, if altmetrics adds little to the existing picture, then there is little justification for expending much time and effort in expanding their use. The converse is that if altmetrics can rightly claim to add value over the use of trad-metrics we would expect it to capture a different perspective from that revealed by its traditional counterparts. If, however, altmetrics is substantively different from its predecessors, it risks losing credibility and being discredited. Resolution of this paradox may come not by attaining greater validity but lie in other advantages, e.g. the facility to derive an earlier picture of quality distinctions or to predict the eventual performance of an article via altmetrics.

A further irony is that the altmetric community seeks to establish credibility by mimicking its forebears. Thus, in 2008 the well-regarded *Journal of Medical Internet Research* began publishing metrics on both views and tweets. On the basis of a reasonably good indication of highly cited articles, Eysenbach (2011) proposed a 'Twimpact factor' (number of tweets an article receives in the first seven days of publication) and a 'Twindex' (the rank percentile of an article's Twimpact factor). Although imitation may be the sincerest form of flattery, altmetrics may prosper more from developing unique and creative ways of demonstrating impact rather than by slavishly imitating the terminology or methodology of traditional metrics.

Some tentative conclusions

Brembs, Button and Munafò (2013) conclude with the pessimistic verdict: 'Given the data we surveyed above [i.e. about journal ranking systems], almost anything appears superior to the status quo.' Harnad (2008) examines whether traditional metrics will continue to have a role in a world that is increasingly populated by social media and social networks. To take just one example, namely download counts (Hitchcock et al., 2003), these are rightly considered a metric of computer activity, not scholarship. Downloads may not be read. Their function may be analogous to downloads of music when compared to live streaming. Just as a single music track may be played multiple times without registering statistics, so too an article may experience multiple use without being captured by metrics. Furthermore, multiple versions of the same article, e.g. publisher and repository versions, may cause counting anomalies analogous to those previously experienced by journals with both print and electronic versions of the same article.

Given the flaws associated with traditional metrics identified from the published research, along with often damning verdicts pronounced by informed critics of the metrics and the academic community at large, it is tempting to sound a death knell for the measures of the immediate past. However, as already stated, and as will become clear from the remainder of this book, the new generation of altmetrics is neither a more accurate representation of academic 'quality' nor immune to criticism.

Interesting results from research seek to isolate the respective values of traditional and altmetrics. For example, a study in *International Journal of Cardiology* compared a top 20 most-cited articles based on downloads from the journal with a top 20 of most-cited articles from the same journal (Coats, 2005). There was no overlap between the two lists. Perneger (2004) studied a cohort of papers published in the *British Medical Journal* in 1999, finding that the hit count on the website in the week after online publication predicted the number of citations in subsequent years. A more recent study (Lokker et al., 2008) confirmed that the citation performance of journal articles can be predicted extremely early, even within three weeks of publication.

What can we conclude from the above? First, although the prevailing opinion is that use of *metrics* is intended to reflect quality, we should not be oblivious to the fact that *choice* of metrics reflects how quality is contemporaneously perceived. A move towards increased use of simple download statistics would offer a strident statement that popularity is one important arbiter of quality; a verdict open to immediate challenge from anyone who compares the top 40 bestselling music tracks of the year with a selection for the same year from informed music critics. Second, lack of consistency between different measures, such as downloads and citations, is not a problem but an opportunity – an opportunity to reflect a more holistic and nuanced appreciation of what academic quality really means. Of course, selection of which metrics are to be used for which purpose – for evaluating an individual, a team or a journal – does not become less problematic, even if the improved ease and sophistication with which such data is collected moves us away from invidious either/or choice scenarios. Finally, in a book that seeks to address an imbalance between long-established traditional metrics and up-and-coming altmetrics, it is hopefully not too subversive to extend a plea for the use of both sets side by side in a display of what I shall label 'complemetrics'!

Key points

- Traditional metrics have tended to focus at the level of the individual, the research team or institution, or the journal.
- All traditional metrics possess significant limitations, are targets for 'game playing' and have been misused in ways that are detrimental to their credibility.
- Altmetrics offers a mechanism by which our conception of impact is usefully expanded, particularly in accelerating the time period within which impact can be detected and tracked.
- Future consensus on the altmetrics of choice, if ever possible(!), may reveal more about contemporaneous attitudes to 'quality' than the inherent value of that particular metric.
- Overall, we foresee altmetrics fulfilling a complementary role with, rather than superseding, that offered by traditional metrics.

Note

1 Unless specifically mentioned, 'metrics' is used to include both bibliometrics and, more broadly, scientometrics, although most examples used in this chapter derive from the former.

References

Agrawal, A. (2005) Corruption of Journal Impact Factors, *Trends in Ecology and Evolution*, **20** (4), 157.

Albuquerque, U. P. (2010) The Tyranny of the Impact Factor: why do we still want to be subjugated?, *Rodriguésia-Instituto de Pesquisas Jardim Botânico do Rio de Janeiro*, **61** (3), 353–8.

Arnold, D. N. and Fowler, K. K. (2011) Nefarious Numbers, *Notices of the American Mathematical Society*, **58** (3), 434–7.

Bain, C. R. and Myles, P. S. (2005) Relationship Between Journal Impact Factor and Levels of Evidence in Anaesthesia, *Anaesthesia and Intensive Care*, **33** (5), 567–70.

Bence, V. and Oppenheim, C. (2005) The Evolution of the UK's Research Assessment Exercise: publications, performance and perceptions, *Journal of Educational Administration and History*, **37** (2), 137–55.

Boyer, E. L. (1990) *Scholarship Reconsidered: priorities of the professoriate*, Princeton, NJ, Carnegie Foundation for the Advancement of Teaching.

Brembs, B., Button, K. and Munafò, M. (2013) Deep Impact: unintended consequences of journal rank, *Frontiers in Human Neuroscience*, **7**, 291.

Button, K. S., Ioannidis, J. P. A., Mokrysz, C., Nosek, B. A., Flint, J., Robinson, E. S. J. et al. (2013) Power Failure: why small sample size undermines the reliability of neuroscience, *National Review of Neuroscience*, **14**, 365–76.

Callaham, M., Wears, R. L. and Weber, E. (2002) Journal Prestige, Publication Bias, and Other Characteristics Associated with Citation of Published Studies in Peer-reviewed Journals, *JAMA*, **287** (21), 2847–50.

Chapman, S., Nguyen, T. N. and White, C. (2007) Press-released Papers Are More Downloaded and Cited, *Tobacco Control*, **16** (1), 71.

Coats, A. J. S. (2005) Top of the Charts: download versus citations in the International Journal of Cardiology, *International Journal of Cardiology*, **105** (2), 123–5.

Colquhoun, D. (2003) Challenging the Tyranny of Impact Factors, *Nature*, **423** (6939), 479.

de Lacey, G., Record, C. and Wade, J. (1985) How Accurate Are Quotations and References in Medical Journals?, *British Medical Journal (Clinical Research Edition)*, **291** (6499), 884–6.

Delamothe, T. and Smith, R. (2004) Open Access Publishing Takes Off, *British Medical Journal*, **328**, 1–3.

Deutsche Forschungsgemeinschaft (DFG) German Research Foundation, press

release, www.dfg.de/en/service/press/press_releases/2010/
pressemitteilung_nr_07/ind [Accessed 17 October 2014].

Dimitrov, J. D., Kaveri, S. V. and Bayry, J. (2010) Metrics: journal's impact
factor skewed by a single paper, *Nature*, **466** (7303), 179.

Dobell, C. (1938) Dr O. Uplavici (1887–1938), *Parasitology*, **30**, 239–41.

EASE (European Association of Science Editors) (2007) Statement on
Inappropriate Use of Impact Factors, Reading: European Association of
Science Editors.

Elsevier (2014) Elsevier Announces Enhanced Journal Metrics SNIP and SJR
Now Available in Scopus, press release, Elsevier [Accessed27 July 2014].

Eysenbach, G. (2011) Can Tweets Predict Citations? Metrics of social impact
based on Twitter and correlation with traditional metrics of scientific
impact, *Journal of Medical Internet Research*, **13** (4), e123. doi: 10.2196/
jmir.2012.

Fassoulaki, A., Papilas, K., Paraskeva, A. and Patris, K. (2002) Impact Factor
Bias and Proposed Adjustments for Its Determination, *Acta
Anaesthesiologica Scandinavica*, **46** (7), 902–5.

Garfield, E. (1994) *The Thomson Reuters Impact Factor*, Thomson Reuters,
20 June.

Garfield, E. (1998) The Impact Factor and Using It Correctly, *Der Unfallchirurg*,
101 (6), 413–4.

Grant, B. (2010) New Impact Factors Yield Surprises, *The Scientist*, 21 June,
www.the-scientist.com/?articles.view/articleNo/29093/title/New-impact-
factors-yield-surprises/(21 June).

Haeffner-Cavaillon, N. and Graillot-Gak, C. (2009) The Use of Bibliometric
Indicators to help Peer-review Assessment, *Archivum Immunologiae et
Therapiae Experimentalis (Warszawa)*, **57**, 33–8. doi: 10.1007/s00005-009-0004-2.

Harnad, S. (2008) Validating Research Performance Metrics Against Peer
Rankings, *Ethics in Science and Environmental Politics*, **8** (11), 103–7.

Harzing, A. and van der Wal, R. (2008) Google Scholar as a new source for
citation analysis, *Ethics in Science and Environmental Politics*, **8** (1), 61–73.

Hirsch, J. E. (2005) An Index to Quantify an Individual's Scientific Research
Output, *Proceedings of the National Academy of Sciences*, **102** (46), 16569–72,
www.pnas.org/cgi/content/abstract/102/46/16569

Hitchcock, S., Woukeu, A., Brody, T., Carr, L., Hall, W. and Harnad, S. (2003)
*Evaluating Citebase, an Open Access Web-based Citation-ranked Search and
Impact Discovery Service*, http://eprints.ecs.soton.ac.uk/8204/.

Joint Committee on Quantitative Assessment of Research (2008) *Citation Statistics* (PDF), International Mathematical Union, 12 June, www.mathunion.org/fileadmin/IMU/Report/CitationStatistics.pdf.

Kjaergard, L. L. and Gluud, C. (2002) Citation Bias of Hepato-biliary Randomized Clinical Trials, *Journal of Clinical Epidemiology*, **55** (4), 407–10.

Lau, S. L. and Samman, N. (2007) Levels of Evidence and Journal Impact Factor in Oral and Maxillofacial Surgery, *International Journal of Oral and Maxillofacial Surgery*, **36** (1), 1–5.

Lokker, C., McKibbon, K., McKinlay, R. J., Wilczynski, N. L. and Haynes, R. B. (2008) Prediction of Citation Counts for Clinical Articles at Two Years Using Data Available within Three Weeks of Publication: retrospective cohort study, *British Medical Journal*, **336** (7645), 655–7.

Lozano, G. A., Larivière, V. and Gingras, Y. (2012) The Weakening Relationship between the Impact Factor and Papers' Citations in the Digital Age, *Journal of the American Society for Information Science and Technology*, **63** (11), 2140.

MacRoberts, M. H. and MacRoberts, B. R. (1989) Problems of Citation Analysis: a critical review, *Journal of the American Society for Information Science*, **40** (5), 342–9.

Moed, H. (2010) Measuring Contextual Citation Impact of Scientific Journals, *Journal of Informetrics*, **4**, 256–77.

Monastersky, R. (2005) The Number That's Devouring Science, *The Chronicle of Higher Education*, **52** (8), 14.

Moustafa, K. (2014) The Disaster of the Impact Factor, *Science and Engineering Ethics*, **21** (1), 139–42.

Nature (2005) Not-so-deep Impact, *Nature*, **435** (7045), 1003–4. doi: 10.1038/4351003b.

Obremskey, W. T., Pappas, N., Attallah-Wasif, E., Tornetta, P. and Bhandari, M. (2005) Level of Evidence in Orthopaedic Journals, *The Journal of Bone & Joint Surgery, American Volume*, **87**, 2632–8.

Opatrný, T. (2008) Playing the System to Give Low-impact Journal More Clout, *Nature*, **455** (7210), 167.

Perneger, T. V. (2004) Relation between Online 'Hit Counts'and Subsequent Citations: prospective study of research papers in the BMJ, *British Medical Journal*, **329** (7465), 546–7.

PLoS Medicine Editors (2006) The Impact Factor Game, *PLoS Medicine*, **3** (6), 6 June, e291.

Reedijk, J. (1998) Sense and Nonsense of Science Citation Analyses: comments on the monopoly position of ISI and citation inaccuracies, risks of possible misuse and biased citation and impact data, *New Journal of Chemistry*, **22** (8), 767–70.

Rossner, M., Van Epps, H. and Hill, E. (2007) Show Me the Data, *Journal of Cell Biology*, **179** (6), 1091–2.

Sahel, J. A. (2011) Quality Versus Quantity: assessing individual research performance, *Science Translational Medicine*, **3** (84), 84cm13.

Schoonbaert, D. and Roelants, G. (1996) Citation Analysis for Measuring the Value of Scientific Publications: quality assessment tool or comedy of errors?, *Tropical Medicine & International Health*, **1** (6), 739–52.

Seglen, P. O. (1997) Why the Impact Factor of Journals Should Not Be Used for Evaluating Research, *British Medical Journal*, **314** (7079), 497.

Simkin, M. V. and Roychowdhury, V. P. (2003) Read before You Cite!, *Complex Systems*, **14**, 269–74

Smith, R. (1997) Journal Accused of Manipulating Impact Factor, *British Medical Journal*, **314** (7079), 461.

Tressoldi, P. E., Giofré, D., Sella, F. and Cumming, G. (2013) High Impact = High Statistical Standards? Not necessarily so, *PloS One*, **8** (2), e56180.

van Raan, A. F. (2003) The Use of Bibliometric Analysis in Research Performance Assessment and Monitoring of Interdisciplinary Scientific Developments, *Technikfolgenabschätzung*, **12** (1), 20–9, English translation available: www.itas.fzk.de/tatup/031/raan03a.htm.

van Raan, A. J. F. (2005) Fatal Attraction: conceptual and methodological issues problems in the ranking of universities by bibliometric methods, *Scientometrics*, **62** (1), 133–43.

West, R. and McIlwaine, A. (2002) What Do Citation Counts Count for in the Field of Addiction? An empirical evaluation of citation counts and their link with peer ratings of quality, *Addiction*, **97** (5), 501–4.

Wilhite, A. W. and Fong, E. A. (2012) Coercive Citation in Academic Publishing, *Science*, **335** (6068), 542–3.

Further reading

Lapinski, S., Piwowar, H. and Priem, J. (2013) Riding the Crest of the Altmetrics Wave: how librarians can help prepare faculty for the next generation of research impact metrics, *College & Research Libraries News*,

74 (6), 292–300.

Lozano, G. A., Larivière, V., Gingras, Y. (2012) The Weakening Relationship between the Impact Factor and Papers' Citations in the Digital Age, *Journal of the American Society for Information Science and Technology*, **63** (11), 2140.

Marcella, R., Lockerbie, H. and Cameron, R. (2015) The Challenge of Demonstrating the Impact of Research beyond Traditional Mechanisms. In *European Conference on Research Methodology for Business and Management Studies*, June 2015, Academic Conferences International Limited.

Penfield, T., Baker, M. J., Scoble, R. and Wykes, M. C. (2013) Assessment, Evaluations, and Definitions of Research Impact: a review, *Research Evaluation*, rvt021, 1–12.

Piwowar, H. (2013) Introduction Altmetrics: what, why and where?, *Bulletin of the American Society for Information Science and Technology*, **39** (4), 8–9.

Roemer, R. C. and Borchardt, R. (2015) *Meaningful Metrics: a 21st century librarian's guide to bibliometrics, altmetrics, and research impact*, Association of College & University Libraries.

CHAPTER 4

The evolution of library metrics

Ben Showers

Have you heard the parable of the man who lost his car keys? Walking to his car from the office in the dark he fumbles for the keys to open the door, and drops them in the gutter. But the light in the gutter is poor, so he undertakes his search on the pavement, where the light from the streetlight is brighter and it's easier to see.

Unable to find his keys, he ends up walking home.

Introduction

We often look for information to help us answer our questions (or find our car keys) in the places where it is easiest to look, where information is easiest to find, even if it isn't the right information to answer our particular questions. The 'streetlight effect' (Freedman, 2010) means that we end up focusing our time and attention on the information and data we discover: how we can make it better, find more of it and so on. We forget the questions that we originally wanted to answer. We are so busy looking where the light is good that we forget what we were looking for and why it was important.

The streetlight effect reminds us that just because we have information it doesn't mean that it is the right information, or that it is telling us what we really want to know. There is also little benefit in collecting all this information – like searching in the light – if, in the end, you find little that you can actually use. If you can't act on the information to inform and improve what you are doing, what is the rationale for collecting all this information? If you're not going to find your keys where the light is good, there is little point in looking there.

Increasingly the scholarly community understands that what we measure should be what is most important to us. Yet the most important things are often obscured by poor light. As research increasingly migrates to the web, with both online journals and more informal channels such as Twitter, blogs and Facebook, what we measure is changing as well. It no longer makes sense for us to base our metrics solely on previous standards of success – such as the number of times an article is cited in other articles – if increasingly we also value tweets or likes, or a quote in a Wikipedia article. In an online, connected and open model of scholarship we need to be constantly revising and revisiting what, how and why we measure and what success means for libraries, researchers and institutions.

This chapter explores the tools and approaches that libraries use to measure what really matters: to them, the institution and researchers, students and staff. Specifically we will look at the metrics that seek to measure and demonstrate the library's impact and value to the institution, academics and its students. We begin by taking a look at what (and how) academic libraries have traditionally measured and how those metrics are changing. As the metrics have changed, so too has the role of the library within the institution. Indeed, as the institutional importance of new areas such as learning analytics and innovative uses of impact data grow, so too the library finds itself strategically positioned to help participate in, or lead, this important area. Few services in the academic institution can claim a familiarity with metrics close to that of the library. Indeed, it has been the library that has played a significant role in introducing notions of impact and value metrics to institutions, students and researchers.

The emergence of value and impact metrics

In 1968 Lloyd and Martha Kramer (Kramer and Kramer, 1968) asked an apparently straightforward question: Does a student's use of the college library have a relationship to the likelihood of that student completing her course and graduating? Such a question appears somewhat unnecessary – of course it does. Doesn't it?

As it happens, the Kramers' paper suggests that there is a statistically significant correlation between library use and 'student persistence'. But, more importantly, the Kramers' and a small handful of other early studies (such as Barkey, 1965, who explored the impact of the library on a student's grade point average) wanted to provide evidence to back up the intuitive responses that such questions usually inspire. They wanted to use the data from the library and other parts of the university (such as the university's registry) to explore whether there was indeed a correlation between library use and student attainment and retention.

So, the desire to use data to determine the impact and value of the library isn't new. However, despite the promise of such early enquiries, for the majority of libraries and their institutions, impact and value are demonstrated through the use of techniques such as satisfaction surveys both locally and nationally (the National Student Survey, or NSS, being the most well known in the UK) and individual student and researcher feedback. These are, of course, valid tools, but they also provide only a small part of the picture. More importantly, these methods also tend to lack the impact of hard numbers and data. This is especially the case when using surveys to present to senior managers who are using the data to decide on the allocation of budgets and precious resources.

In contrast, the emergence of research metrics has been marked by its use of a powerfully simple numeric and quantitative approach. Initially, at least, research metrics had little to do with providing data for the researchers themselves. Rather, they provided the institution and the library with a quantitative means to evaluate the value and impact of content, specifically scholarly journals. Librarians and information scientists have been evaluating academic journals for as long as journals have been part of the library collection (early 20th-century examples include Gross and Gross's analysis of citation patterns in the 1920s). The most important development in the quantitative evaluation of journal impact was Eugene Garfield's impact factor. A journal's impact factor is a measure of the average number of citations of articles published in that journal. Garfield's idea that citations can help to define the importance and value of a source has had a huge and ongoing influence;

it can be seen in Google's Pagerank algorithm, for example. The impact factor is a relatively recent addition to what is termed bibliometrics, or the application of statistical and mathematical analysis of written publications, such as articles and books (Wikipedia: http://en.wikipedia. org/wiki/Bibliometrics).

Indeed, we might argue that libraries have largely been responsible for introducing scholars to many of the metrics that they use today. For example, the journal impact factor – a set of proprietary metrics developed by Thomson Reuters based on the work of Garfield – was, in the 1980s, embedded in the Web of Knowledge platform to which libraries provided access for academics and researchers. This provided access not only to the content, but also to the metrics by which the value and impact of that content was being judged. What started as a peripheral part of the content that libraries provide has grown in significance and importance in its own right.

The past few decades have seen the field of bibliometrics flourish. Accompanying the journal impact factor in recent years have been a number of other bibliometric indicators, including the h index, which measures the citations for a specific researcher's publications, the Eigen factor, which aims to score a journal's importance, and the g index, which quantifies productivity based on publication record. Not only has the spread of these measures increased, but they have also become entrenched in academic culture, so much so that when the UK's Research Excellence Framework (REF) – which aims to assess the quality of research in UK higher education institutions – forbade its subject review panels to use the journal impact factor and other journal rankings, informal polls and research suggested that these were still, overwhelmingly, being used (see, for example, Rohn, 2012).

Not only have librarians used bibliometrics as a part of their own strategic toolkit (to support purchasing decisions or provide evidence for relegating or disposing of journal runs), but these have also been a key part of services that libraries provide to researchers and academics. Beyond helping to shape collection management policies and strategy, these metrics have also formed a core part of the evolving role of research and academic support provided by librarians. Bibliometrics are part of the work that librarians undertake to help support and guide researchers, from enabling them to better understand and track their own impact through to increasing digital literacy and improving research methods (see, for example, Delasale, 2011).

The ability of the impact factor and bibliometrics in general to provide a single quantitative figure for the impact of a journal and, increasingly, a researcher makes it very attractive. But impact indicators have become so seductive that they are threatening scholarly communication itself.

This single number, the impact factor, is devouring science.

A fixation on measuring

Indeed, impact factors have assumed so much power, especially in the past five years, that they are starting to control the scientific enterprise.

(Monastersky, 2005)

It wasn't meant to be like this. Garfield's idea was meant to be a way for him to pick out the most important scientific journals and distinguish them from the lesser ones. It was a tool that, as we have seen, has uses from informing library collection and purchasing decisions through to helping researchers to make decisions about which journal to publish in. As Garfield himself said: 'We never predicted that people would turn this into an evaluation tool for giving out grants and funding' (Monastersky, 2005).

As these metrics became accessible online, so their influence grew. Indeed, it is an influence that seems to be affecting the very types of research and science that are being conducted. As mentioned earlier, higher-impact journals tend to favour more fashionable and 'sexy subjects' (Schekman, 2013). It is the impact factor – as the exemplar research metric – that in the online world has seen its ubiquity and power grow to almost pestilential levels. It is beginning to have a 'toxic influence' on scholarly discourse and communication (Sample, 2013). As we have already seen with the UK REF example, attempts to reduce or remove the influence of the impact factor from assessments tend to have little effect. The impact factor is deeply embedded in institutional culture, helping to determine promotions and funding. It has also led to accusations that it encourages researchers to explore fashionable topics favoured by high-impact journals, and the charge that journals and publishers are gaming the system in order to inflate their own rankings (see, for example, Wilhite and Fong, 2012).

It is the web that has provided the impact factor and research metrics with greater visibility and influence (for more information on both how the web has impacted on research metrics and the failings of research metrics in general, see Chapter 3 in this volume). But that increased visibility has sown the seeds of the impact factor's own demise. Not only does research in a web-based world demand new and better metrics, but it also bestows on researchers, students, institutions and libraries the ability to develop their own metrics, to measure what's most important to them, and to get the data and tools they need to influence those things for the better.

A new metrics frontier

We are experiencing a great migration; scholarly workflows, debates and outputs are increasingly taking place online, on web-based spaces such as blogs, Twitter, Facebook, Wikipedia and so on. Such a migration challenges the very conventions of what research and scholarship looks like. Stated simply, research on the web no longer needs to conform to the physical boundaries of a printed journal volume. It need not have a clearly defined beginning or end – it can be an ongoing scholarly conversation. It can have the underlying data embedded in the article or it can include media such as video or music. It need not even be an article; it could be a blog post, a video, a presentation or a series of tweets. The possibilities are endless and help to disrupt our current notions of scholarship and scholarly communication.

Connected to this sense that the boundaries of scholarship and its outputs are changing is the facility for us to make visible what was once hidden. With every page view, followed link or tweeted paper we are leaving a visible trace of our interactions with an article or academic output. Furthermore, even the very embryonic beginnings of a piece or area of research can be traced. Initial discussions between colleagues that would once have remained hidden can be traced across the web through blog posts and comments or a series of tweets. While scholarly communications have been slow to fully utilize the potential of the web, the web has had the effect of making what were once 'backstage' activities visible. It has led to these activities increasingly being 'tagged, catalogued, and archived on blogs, Mendeley, Twitter, and elsewhere' (Priem, 2011).

Understanding these new and emerging data sources and how they might inform scholarly and impact metrics has become known as altmetrics. Altmetrics is the various and diverse indicators that help scholars and institutions to see what impact looks like. As the Altmetrics Manifesto states: 'Altmetrics expand our view of what impact looks like, but also of what's making the impact' (Priem et al., 2010).

Libraries have been instrumental in helping to shape altmetrics and disseminate it to the researcher community. This role has solidified in recent years as new products, services and platforms have emerged to support the use of altmetrics in academia. These services and tools include, for example: Impactstory (http://impactstory.org), Plum Analytics (www.plumanalytics.com) and Altmetric.com (www.altmetric.com). The creation of these institution-friendly tools is helping to drive the adoption of these services and providing an important counterbalance to the powerful hold of traditional research metrics within academia.

Yet, ironically, many of these alternative metrics are deeply embedded in the previous metrics paradigm. As Andrew Booth makes clear in Chapter 3 of this volume,' A further irony is that the altmetric community seeks to establish credibility by mimicking its forebears.' Yet, the library continues to play a role in the development and ongoing adoption of more diverse metrics and analysis. This exploration of new types of metrics is also rooted in the past, in capturing the library's impact and contribution to student success. In understanding the library's impact on teaching and learning we are beginning to see the start of a 'turn' in the library's approach to metrics.

The analytics turn in libraries

As we saw earlier, the interest for libraries in how they contribute to the success of their students isn't new.

Over the last few years libraries, in particular academic libraries, have been developing more sophisticated and data-driven approaches to demonstrating the impact of library services and resources to the host institution and beyond. In particular, since the turn of the 21st century, there has been an increasing amount of literature on the impact of libraries on their users, literature that is using data to demonstrate the value of libraries to their users. This work has explored the relationship of the library and its resources and space to the performance of students. Early work tended to take place in an environment where print was still dominant (De Jager, 2002) and at a time when extracting and sharing data from library and institutional systems was difficult and time consuming. Some, from the public library sector (Sin and Kim, 2008; Suaiden, 2003), explored wider societal impacts and demographic usage patterns.

From around 2010 onwards there was a resurgence of data-driven strategy and analytics within the academic library sector. In particular there has been significant and ground-breaking work by universities in the UK, USA and Australia to see how the myriad data that flows through libraries and wider institutions can be harnessed for the benefit of students and researchers. The libraries at the universities of Huddersfield in the UK, Wollongong in Australia and Minnesota in the USA are gathering and analysing data both from the library and from across external enterprise systems to demonstrate the value that they bring to the wider life of the institution and the success of their students and researchers (for case studies of these three projects see Showers, 2015).

What marks out this work from previous attempts is the diversity of data that is being collected: the libraries are interested in data from across their systems and services (gate count, e-resource usage, computer logins) as well as from across the institution (student records, student services, registry, IT). Taken together, these data sets are more powerful than they would be individually. But this diverse data isn't collected for its own sake or because it's easy to get. Rather, it is selected and tested to ensure that it is able to provide real insights – insights that can then be acted on. It tells the library something that it can respond to; it is actionable data (the data might, for example, highlight differences in how the library is used at certain times, allowing the library to tailor services for specific times of the day). And, finally, the data isn't just about helping to improve the user experience for existing services and systems. It is also being used to help develop and underpin new types of services and interventions. These new services can be more intimately tailored to the needs of users, or groups of users, increasing the value of those services and of the library overall.

It is worth looking briefly at the work led in the UK by the University of Huddersfield. The Library Impact Data Project (LIDP), funded by Jisc, looked at data from over 33,000 undergraduate students from across eight universities. The project aimed to test the hypothesis that there is a statistical significance across a number of universities between library activity data and student attainment/achievement, although it is important to note that this relationship is not causal. The project was able to support the hypothesis (Stone et al., 2012) and was supported by similar studies in Australia (Cox and Jantti, 2012; Jantti and Cox, 2013) and the USA (Nackerud et al., 2013).

The success of the LIDP work led to a second phase of the project that examined data from 3000 full-time undergraduates from the University of Huddersfield. This phase used continuous rather than categorical data, which allowed the project to do more with the data. The aim of the study was to dig deeper into the data and look at a number of new data categories, such as demographic information, discipline, retention, on- and off-campus use, breadth and depth of e-resource usage and UCAS (University and College Admissions Service) data (Stone and Collins, 2013). Using students' final grades as a percentage, rather than a class, also allowed phase 2 to demonstrate a correlation in the phase 1 hypothesis, in addition to the statistical significance found in phase 1 (further strengthening the findings from phase 1 of the study).

What these projects have helped to demonstrate is that not only does the library play a critical role in the life and success of its students but also, increasingly, libraries are keen to make sure that they can analyse the data they have in their systems and services to help improve those services and systems. This data is enabling libraries to set entirely new metrics for what success looks like and, as a result of effective data analysis, new types of service and interventions are beginning to emerge. Indeed, as the work led by Huddersfield has demonstrated, much of the benefit of analysing data comes when you are able to aggregate large amounts of data, from diverse sources, across different institutions.

Shared analytics and metrics services

Libraries have a long and successful history of collaborating and sharing services and systems at regional, sector and national levels. In the UK such services are exemplified by, among others, the Journal Usage Statistics Portal (JUSP; http://jusp.mimas.ac.uk/) for journal usage data, Institutional Repository Usage Statistics (IRUS; www.irus.mimas.ac.uk) for repository usage statistics and COPAC collections management (http://copac.ac.uk/innovations/collections-management), a shared collections management tool that allows libraries to compare their local collection against other libraries in the UK, thereby informing library collection policies about what might be relegated and also to support purchase decisions.

These services highlight that the data libraries collect and the metrics used should be primarily focused on enabling the library to act on that data. Increasingly, we need to move to a model where the data, and to some extent the analysis, is available at the 'push of a button' (or as near to that as possible). The focus of resources and energies should be on acting on the data, not collecting it.

Building on this appetite for shared data services and the innovative work on library impact led by the University of Huddersfield, Jisc funded the Library Analytics and Metrics Project (LAMP) to develop a shared national service to enable institutions and libraries to make sense of their disparate and diverse data sets and enable them to spend their precious time and resources acting on these data-driven insights to improve the student and researcher experience (Showers and Stone, 2014). Working with eight institutional partners, the project is ingesting a variety of library and institutional data in order to clean and normalize the data and present it back to the library via an intuitive data dashboard. The prototype aims both to remove a lot of the burden of collecting disparate data sets and to do some of the initial analysis.

LAMP will use the opportunities of scale to access a much larger number of datasets, analysable both at the local, institutional level and at the shared, above-campus level. In both cases it is hoped to gain new insights, such as on national usage patterns, and to enhance services and functionality for institutions, such as benchmarking and personalization. Such an approach might enable both very localized, individual insights, such as alerts for students who may be at risk of failing their course or for a cohort of students who need specialized services, and national measures of what success looks like. Indeed, it is possible to imagine services like LAMP being able to work with projects such as those in Australia (Wollongong) and the USA (Minnesota) to begin establishing international benchmarks for their libraries. In an increasingly international education environment, such an approach may become a necessity.

Like altmetrics, many of these shared library analytics services, as exemplified by LAMP, offer the potential for libraries to increasingly tailor their services and systems to the individual user. By filtering the open web, altmetrics presents the potential for personalized information flows. By understanding user interactions with the library and its services, shared analytics and data services enable better and more intimate services for their users.

The evolution of library metrics is inevitably drawing us toward a position where we are delving ever more deeply into data for nuanced insights. This means that libraries must explore mixed methods; we must measure and count, as well as ask open-ended questions. We are witnessing the beginnings of a rebalancing of the data and analytics methodology: a rebalancing that incorporates ways that enable the user to tell their own story. The role of the librarian, archivist or curator is to listen and, when appropriate, to question the narrative; this is, after all, an active dialogue with the user, not passive listening.

Listening to the user

A mixed-methods approach, where both quantitative and qualitative approaches are taken, enables the library service to understand what the user actually does and the context for those actions and the experience that those interactions provide. This coalescence of data is incredibly powerful, both for understanding how current services are used and might be improved and also for articulating hidden or emerging needs and requirements that users themselves may not be entirely aware of. For example, the way that we interact with a space may leave traces of a need that could never be fully articulated by the user. Yet, should that space be altered to meet that nascent need, the user's experience might be positively transformed.

Donna Lanclos is an anthropologist who works at the University of North Carolina, Charlotte, as the library's ethnographer. She blogs at Anthropologist in the Stacks (http://atkinsanthro.blogspot.co.uk) and has a role that ensures that the decisions the library makes about services, systems and space are all anchored by the behaviours, practices and motivations of the students at the institution.

Donna's work covers a lot of different areas, including space planning. Her work has explored how students use a 24-hour library space late at night and early in the morning. Unsurprisingly, or maybe surprisingly, a significant amount of that usage is for students' sleeping. Donna's work has involved her in mapping the areas that students prefer for sleeping in, so as to understand how the library can redesign those spaces to take such behaviours into account. It doesn't have to be students slumped on desks (Lanclos, 2013)!

Understanding how students interact and engage with library space means that the library can respond to how students *actually* engage and behave, rather than how it wishes or would like students to engage.

Similar kinds of insight are also required for online, web-based interactions. Longitudinal research into student behaviours, such as the visitors and residents approach (JISC, 2014), provides critical insights into the behaviours of students in a digital information environment as they progress through the educational system (from school to postgraduate). The visitors and residents work is already challenging the assumptions we have about how students behave in an online environment, and how they learn and collaborate, and is identifying new modes of engagement such as 'learning black markets' (White, 2011). In terms of the learning black market, for example, the work uncovers the informal and peripheral collaborations and studying that take place just beyond the formal structures and services of the institution. Here activities might include using Facebook to collaborate on an essay, and the use of sources such as Wikipedia and the interrogation of those sources through online messaging or text messaging, for example. There may be opportunities for the library and other services to support students in understanding and interrogating sources when these informal activities might intersect with more formal institutional activities (such as researching for an essay). These may not be the traditional forms of support offered by the library, but they are ones that have the potential to transform the students' experience. They also ask serious questions of whether the library and institution should even be engaging in these informal spaces of the students. Is this a space that should remain beyond the reach of formal interventions?

By itself this analytics data provides only a part of the overall story. Analytics data is very effective for telling you *what* your users are doing, and quite possibly *how* they are doing it. But what it cannot tell you is *why* they are doing it.

It is the 'why' that also opens up the possibility of identifying new potential services and interventions that can meet undeclared user needs and transform the experience of users. More fundamentally, the ethnographic and mixed-methods approaches described in this chapter place the user at the heart of developments. Increasingly, our metrics for success depend not just on numbers but also on a narrative from the user or visitor that includes words such as 'delightful', 'surprising' and 'amazing'.

Conclusion

What was once hidden or obscure is increasingly visible. The invisible traces of an academic reading an unpublished paper, or of students collaborating online for an essay due in the following day, are increasingly the places and spaces that suggest the boundaries of the new metrics frontier for libraries and academic institutions.

The academic library is ideally placed to be a key partner or strategic lead in this emerging area. Libraries are accustomed to measuring things. Some of these you'd expect: numbers of users, number of downloads, the amount of available shelf space. Some you might not, such as quantifying the value that the library contributes to student success or recording the number of users sleeping in the library (and where they are sleeping). Indeed, it is the academic library that has so often been at the forefront of attempts to measure what is important for the university, its students and staff and the library itself to understand and to change for the better.

As the evolution of impact and value metrics has demonstrated, the library is ideally positioned to challenge and question over-reliance on any one form of metric or method of analysis. Indeed, as the library has developed metrics to ensure that the user sits at the heart of any metrics developed, so it can provide the same user-centric approach when supporting wider, strategic engagements with learning and research metrics across the institution.

The future of library metrics is about librarians constantly challenging and reassessing the metrics they use to measure the things that are most important to their users and themselves and ensuring that they have the right tools and measures that will shine a light into areas that once seemed impossibly dark, but where the greatest rewards can be uncovered.

Key points

- Library metrics emerged as librarians explored how to demonstrate the impact of the library on the life and success of their users.
- The current abundance of research and scholarly metrics can be traced back to libraries' original interest in their impact on user success (metrics such as the journal impact factor, for example).
- Impact indicators have become so seductive that they are threatening scholarly communication itself. A single metric, the impact factor, is devouring science.
- As scholarship evolves, so too do the kinds of metrics and measures of scholarship. Increasingly, these are focusing on web-based metrics and social indicators of impact (such as 'shares', 'downloads' and 'hits', for example).
- These alternative metrics, or altmetrics, are increasingly popular, with new services and tools emerging to support scholars and institutions in measuring the impact of their work.
- Libraries are once again at the centre of these new developments in scholarly and information metrics. Libraries are both supporting scholars in understanding and measuring their impact and using data-driven approaches to how they themselves undertake their work (such as data-driven collection management).
- In isolation, quantitative methods of measuring impact are insufficient. Instead, libraries and institutions must adopt a mixed methodology that uses quantitative data along with qualitative (ethnographic) data.
- The library is at the heart of much of the current debate and experimentation around metrics and analytics. Libraries therefore have

an opportunity to be at the heart of driving new developments and ensuring that the most important things for its users are being measured.

References

Barkey, P. (1965) Patterns of Student Use of a College Library, *College Research Library*, March (2), 115–18.

Cox, B. and Jantti, M. (2012) Discovering the Impact of Library Use and Student Performance, *Educause Review Online*, July, http://er.educause.edu/articles/2012/7/discovering-the-impact-of-library-use-and-student-performance.

De Jager, K. (2002) Successful Students: does the library make a difference?, *Performance Measurement and Metrics*, **3** (3), 140–4

Delasale, J. (2011) Research Evaluation: bibliometrics and the librarian, *SCONUL Focus*, **53**, 16–19.

Freedman, H. D. (2010) Why Scientific Studies Are So Often Wrong: the streetlight effect, *Discover*, July/August, http://discovermagazine.com/2010/jul-aug/29-why-scientific-studies-often-wrong-streetlight-effect.

Gross, P. L. K. and Gross, E. M. (1927) College Libraries and Chemical Education, *Science*, **66**, 385–9.

Jantti, M. and Cox, B. (2013) Measuring the Value of Library Resources and Student Academic Performance through Relational Datasets, *Evidence Based Library and Information Practice*, **8** (2), 163–71.

Jisc (2014) *Evaluating Digital Services: the visitors and residents approach*, www.jiscinfonet.ac.uk/infokits/evaluating-services/visitors-residents/.

Kramer, L. and Kramer, M. (1968) The College Library and the Drop Out, *College Research Library*, **29**, July, 310–12.

Lanclos, D. (2013) Sleeping and Successful Library Spaces, Anthropologist in the Stacks, http://atkinsanthro.blogspot.co.uk/2013/08/sleeping-and-successful-library-spaces.html.

Monastersky, R. (2005) The Number That's Devouring Science, *Chronicle of Higher Education*, 1 October, http://chronicle.com/article/The-Number-That-s-Devouring/26481.

Nackerud, S. et al. (2013) Analyzing Demographics: assessing library use across the institution, *Libraries and the Academy*, **13** (2), 131–45.

Priem, J. (2011) As Scholars Undertake a Great Migration to Online

Publishing, Altmetrics Stands to Provide an Academic Measurement of Twitter and Other Online Activity, LSE Impact of Social Science Blog, http://blogs.lse.ac.uk/impactofsocialsciences/2011/11/21/altmetrics-twitter.

Priem, J., Taraborelli, D., Groth, P. and Neylon, C. (2010) *Altmetrics: a manifesto*, http://altmetrics.org/manifesto.

Rohn, J. (2012) Business as Usual in Judging the Worth of a Researcher?, *Guardian*, 30 November.

Sample, A. (2013) Nobel Winner Declares Boycott of Top Science Journals, *Guardian*, 9 December.

Schekman, R. (2013) How Journals Like Nature, Cell and Science are Damaging Science, *Guardian*, 9 December.

Showers, B. (2015) *Library Analytics and Metrics: using data to drive decisions and services*, Facet Publishing.

Showers, B. and Stone, G. (2014) Safety in Numbers: developing a shared analytics service for academic libraries, *Performance Measurement and Metrics*, **15** (1/2), 13–22.

Sin, S.-C.J. and Kim, K.-S. (2008) Use and Non-use of Public Libraries in the Information Age: a logistic regression analysis of household characteristics and library services variables, *Library & Information Science Research*, **30** (3), 207–15.

Stone, G. and Collins, E. (2013) Library Usage and Demographic Characteristics of Undergraduate Students in a UK University, *Performance Measurement and Metrics*, **14** (1), 25–35.

Stone, G. et al. (2012) Library Impact Data Project: hit, miss or maybe. In *Proving Value in Challenging Times: Proceedings of the 9th Northumbria International Conference on Performance Measurement in Libraries and Information Services, University of York*, University of York, 385–90.

Suaiden, E. J. (2003) The Social Impact of Public Libraries, *Library Review*, **52** (8), 379–87.

White, D. (2011) *The Learning Black Market*, http://tallblog.conted.ox.ac.uk/index.php/2011/09/30/the-learning-black-market/.

Wilhite, A. W. and Fong, E. A. (2012) Coercive Citation in Academic Publishing, *Science*, **335** (6068), 542–3.

Useful resources and further reading
Articles and books

Piwowar, H. (2013) Introduction Altmetrics: what, why and where?, *Bulletin of the American Society for Information Science and Technology*, **39** (4), 8–9.

Roemer, R. C. and Borchardt, R. (2015) *Meaningful Metrics: a 21st century librarian's guide to bibliometrics, altmetrics, and research impact*, Association of College & University Libraries.

Showers, B. (ed.) (2015) *Library Analytics and Metrics: using data to drive decisions and services*, Facet Publishing.

Library analytics case studies

Discovering the impact of library use and student performance (the Library Cube): http://bit.ly/libcube.

Library data and student success (University of Minnesota): http://bit.ly/MinnImpact.

Library Impact Data Project (LIDP at Huddersfield): http://bit.ly/libimpact.

Toolkits/resources

A useful overview of bibliometrics: http://en.wikipedia.org/wiki/Bibliometrics.

An introduction to web metrics: www.libqual.org/documents/admin/arl_emetrics_workshop_june05.pdf.

Educause Library Analytics Toolkit: www.educause.edu/library/analytics.

Exploiting activity data in the academic environment: www.activitydata.org.

Library analytics bibliography: http://bit.ly/analyticsbib.

CHAPTER 5

The rise of altmetrics

Euan Adie

Introduction

To understand the significance of altmetrics tools and the motivations of their users it is useful for librarians and other information professionals to understand the historical context and primary drivers leading up to the Altmetrics Manifesto.

The Altmetrics Manifesto was published in October 2010 and written by Jason Priem, Dario Taraborelli, Paul Groth and Cameron Neylon. It is described later in this chapter. However, in brief, it drew on earlier work by all four authors and others to suggest that 'the rapid evolution of scholarly communication, the speed, richness, and breadth of altmetrics make them worth investing in', asserting that 'scholarship's [. . .] main filters for importance are failing' and calling for more tools and research into the area.

Around this document the fledgling field of altmetrics coalesced in a remarkably short space of time, driven by a combination of academic research, practical application and increased funding from a variety of sources.

Altmetrics takes at least two 'alternative' (to traditional, citation-based metrics) approaches: widening the definition of research outputs to include more than just books and journal articles, and looking beyond citations for a quantitative way of assessing or discovering them.

One measure of rapid development since the manifesto was

published is the number of journals that have adopted some form of altmetrics display for authors or readers – by mid-2015 this was around 6500 (from internal Altmetric.com data via personal communication), including well-known titles like *Nature, Cell, PLOS ONE, Science* and the *Proceedings of the National Academies of Science*. Another measure may be the number of research articles with a title matching 'altmetrics' found on Google Scholar – more than 300 since the manifesto was first published.

In parallel to these academic research efforts, altmetrics tools have been developed by both commercial companies like Altmetric.com and Elsevier and not-for-profits like the Public Library of Science (PLOS) and Impactstory. As these tools improve and become more useful they drive more interest in the field and become more popular, spreading the ideas and concepts behind the manifesto to wider audiences. At my company, Altmetric.com, the altmetrics data we provide is shown on some 6000 academic journals from 60 different publishers.

To understand where many of these tools come from and why they are suddenly becoming popular – at least relative to most developments in scholarly communication – it's useful to consider four powerful external forces without which the rapid uptake of altmetrics would not have been possible.

The first is the gradual shift of scholarship from the analogue to the digital world, with researchers now discovering, consuming and producing much of their scholarship online.

The second is researcher engagement with the new possibilities that the shift to digital has brought – post-publication review, science blogs, online reference managers and discussion sites – and with Web 2.0 concepts like filter failure, crowdsourcing and the wisdom of crowds, which have been built on and adapted to suit the particular needs of literature discovery and dissemination.

The third is growing interest from funders in 'non-traditional' research outputs like datasets or software, and the expectation that researchers should provide evidence demonstrating the value of their research to society (Dinsmore, Allen and Dolby, 2014).

Fourth, but no less important, is the influence of wider changes in scholarly communications and its infrastructure, particularly changes relating to the open access movement and a shift away from journal-level metrics like the impact factor to metrics collected on an article-by-article basis.

Of course, popularity isn't everything. Early altmetrics tools – from PLOS, Impactstory, Altmetric.com and others – have played an important role in shaping how altmetrics is perceived by researchers, institutions and funders and in helping to kick-start the development of the right processes and controls for their use. This process too has been influenced by the forces mentioned above.

Filter failure

The original Altmetrics Manifesto was concerned mainly with the failure of filters for 'importance' – specifically, peer review, citations and journal-level metrics like the impact factor.

The suggestion was that these more traditional filters work slowly and don't capture a rich enough picture of the different ways in which an article might be important to a consumer of academic research. Furthermore, they focus on articles and book chapters at the expense of more diverse expressions of scholarship like datasets, blogs and code.

It's worth noting that 'importance' is used fairly broadly by the manifesto authors to cover discovery (finding research that one should read), assessment (helping to gauge the quality of research) and impact (in this context the effect that the research has had on the wider world as well as on other research through, for example, reuse of data).

The problem of information overload is familiar to most active internet users. As more and more information comes online – filling up Twitter feeds, RSS readers and news websites – it can become difficult to keep up with it all. But what if the problem isn't too much content per se but, rather, a failure in how we process it? The concept of 'filter failure' comes from a seminal talk given in 2009 by Clay Shirky, a professor of new media at New York University, who suggested:

> What we are dealing with now isn't information overload, because we are always dealing with information overload, the problem is filter failure.
>
> (Shirky, 2009)

Shirky asserted that as the cost of content production falls, so there is a reducing economic reason for content producers to filter for quality. A traditional book publisher picks and chooses what content it publishes, as it needs to ensure that it sells enough copies to recoup costs, but if I create my own blog online I can produce or share as much content as I like – pictures of my cat included – for almost nothing.

Filter failure, then, is a failure to weed out irrelevant or poor-quality content before it hits your inbox, or search results page, or however you consume the content in question.

Researchers are not immune to the issue. As online publishing and dissemination becomes easier there has been an accompanying explosion in the volume of content. In 2012 it was found that an estimated 1.8–1.9 million research articles are published each year worldwide and the number grows by about 3% a year (Ware and Mabe, 2012).

As an academic you need to keep track of what's happening in your own field as well as, ideally, any applicable work in other disciplines, and that may become difficult – or at least uneconomic – to do by reading everything yourself.

The traditional models of filtering by subscribing to a few relevant journals or carrying out keyword searches become untenable as journals and mega-journals (open access titles publishing thousands of articles a year, often across a broad spectrum of subject areas) proliferate and the volume of articles increases.

> The speed of altmetrics presents the opportunity to create real-time recommendation and collaborative filtering systems: instead of subscribing to dozens of tables-of-contents, a researcher could get a feed of this week's most significant work in her field.
>
> (Priem et al., 2010)

Perhaps a better filter, the manifesto suggested, was altmetrics data, the online conversation and discussion surrounding research outputs and driven by researchers themselves.

In 2010, one important question was whether or not there is enough of such research conversation online to be used in any meaningful way. The first of the external forces mentioned above has helped to address this concern.

From analogue to digital scholarship

Altmetrics is to a great degree digital – it typically uses digital resources or events happening online as a proxy for real-world activity. This is possible because since the advent of Web 2.0 in 2004 the way researchers discover, produce, consume and discuss academic outputs has shifted online.

Changes in reference management present a good example of how the shift to online has enabled new data applications, as well as making life easier for end-users.

Before 2005 a researcher's options for managing references were fairly limited. Two products – EndNote and Reference Manager, both owned by Thomson Reuters Corporation – dominated the market. Both ran on the user's local computer and references were private to you, the user.

Social bookmarking presented an opportunity to researchers who were interested in coming up with an alternative (Hull, Pettifer and Kell, 2008), and several new online applications for reference management and sharing became available.

Connotea (now defunct) and CiteULike (www.citeulike.com) were two early offerings. Both used del.icio.us (http://del.icio.us) – a comparatively generic online bookmarks manager which allowed users to tag and describe bookmarks and then share them with others – as a model.

The tools did not emerge from a vacuum, nor were they amateur affairs. Connotea was notable for having been written and maintained by Nature Publishing Group as part of its web publishing initiative in which a variety of new, relatively innovative online applications – including an early social network for scientists, a pre-print server for the life sciences and a blog aggregator – were presented to researchers.

A desire for richer user interfaces led to a shift towards applications run locally but with an online component, allowing users to integrate it with word processors and to manage citation styles and reference lists once they were inserted into text.

Mendeley (www.mendeley.com), described in detail in Chapter 6, is a popular online reference manager. An early feature of Mendeley allowed users to upload PDF documents from their desktop to Mendeley's servers online, from where they could 'sync' their library to a different computer. The PDFs would be analysed, their metadata extracted and articles disambiguated so that the same paper in different PDF versions (for example, with cover pages showing different dates, or author copies) would be treated as a single item.

Mendeley then created a landing page specifically for the paper showing the title, other bibliographic details and a reader count, i.e. the count of how many researchers had that paper in their library.

An obvious next step was to allow the sharing of papers and references within small groups, and Mendeley started to allow this with the introduction of group functionality in 2010. With EndNote, users may have had to share individual papers by e-mail or to share a database file; with Mendeley, they now only had to join the relevant group on the Mendeley website.

Reader counts on Mendeley and associated demographic information have since proved to be a useful – and high-volume – source of altmetrics data. This is reflected in research; three-quarters of the papers in Google Scholar from 2014 with the word 'altmetrics' in the title also contained the word 'Mendeley' in the text.

Altmetrics and the wisdom of crowds

To understand where some of the ideas in the Altmetrics Manifesto came from it's worth taking a step back to see how they tie in with the 'wisdom of crowds', 'crowdsourcing' and 'collaborative filtering' – all concepts that were, like 'filter failure', described and popularized in the 2000s.

Jeff Howe, a contributing editor of *Wired* magazine, coined the term 'crowdsourcing' in 2005, to mean:

> The act of taking a job once performed by a designated agent (an employee, freelancer or a separate firm) and outsourcing it to an undefined, generally large group of people through the form of an open call, which usually takes place over the Internet.
>
> (Safire, 2009)

James Surowiecki, a journalist at the *New York Times*, wrote *The Wisdom of Crowds* in 2004. In this book he argues that by aggregating information from groups of people you can come to decisions that are often better – wiser – than those that would have been made by any one member of that group (Surowiecki, 2004).

Variants of these ideas influenced the manifesto and early altmetrics tools both directly and indirectly. For example del.icio.us (http://del.icio.us), mentioned previously as the model for CiteULike and Connotea, had earlier popularized the notion of 'folksonomy'. The concept is fairly simple: if each person who bookmarks a link can add tags (short descriptive words or phrases) of their own choosing to it, then by looking at all of the tags being assigned (and how frequently each one occurs across different users) a type of flexible, crowd-driven ontology emerges (Haplin, Robu and Shepherd, 2007).

User-driven tagging is now fairly common in information management tools and web applications that accept user-generated content. For example, Tumblr – a popular blogging platform which at the time of writing hosted 225 million different short-form blogs – encourages content creators to tag each of their posts with descriptive terms that other Tumblr users can use to jump from one blog to another on the same topic.

From an altmetrics perspective the success of user tagging and folksonomies reinforced two ideas: first, that useful information can be extracted as a side-effect of interactions with content (users tag content not to create a folksonomy, but for their own benefit), and second, that the information is the more useful the more people are doing the interacting (the more users there are, the more comprehensive the tagging).

To create a folksonomy it's useful for the crowd in question to have a diversity of opinions so as to get a broad spectrum of tags (although there's a flip side to this, which is that, ideally, you want people to express – and spell – discrete concepts the same way). This spectrum is important in collaborative filtering, which is mentioned specifically in the manifesto.

At its simplest, collaborative filtering can be summed up as 'other people who like this also like that'. A machine-learning technique rather than a specific algorithm, it involves making recommendations to you based on the past behaviour of people who share your tastes.

Collaborative filtering for content discovery may be complex or simple. CiteULike presents good examples of both. If I tag a paper from *Nature* with 'drosophila genomics' and then click on that tag I will be taken to a page on the CiteULike system where I can see all the other research papers (across all journals) that people have tagged with the same text. Perhaps there will be something relevant there that I've missed.

However, that might be too broad, and it doesn't necessarily cut down on the number of articles I have to scan through before I see anything relevant. Luckily, CiteULike also offers a more sophisticated collaborative filtering mechanism: recommendations that are based on what people who use the same kind of tags as me are currently saving to their CiteULike libraries. As well as organizing the articles I've already read by tagging them, I'm telling the system with whom I share reading preferences (in this case drosophila genomics researchers) and allowing it to deliver recommendations to me based on its activity.

Researcher engagement with scholarly communications online
Post-publication review

In late 2006 PLoS (now PLOS), a not-for-profit academic publisher, announced that its new journal *PLOS ONE* would publish any research, with traditional peer review limited to whether or not the science was sound. Pulling research from several broad fields and with a high volume of articles put online each week, it was impossible to track new, relevant articles in the way many academics traditionally would, by subscribing to e-mail alerts of the table of contents.

Instead, post-publication review, along with new filters on the journal platform, was encouraged to help people separate the wheat from the chaff.

Every paper submitted to the journal is reviewed by at least one member of *PLOS ONE*'s editorial board of over 200 researchers, but only to check for serious flaws in the way the experiment was conducted and analysed. In contrast to almost all other journals, referees ignore the significance of the result. Notable papers are instead highlighted by the attention they attract after publication.

Visitors to the *PLOS ONE* website can, for example, attach comments to specific parts of a paper and rate the paper as a whole. Data from those systems, as well as download and citation statistics, then allow

PLOS ONE's editors to identify and promote the papers that researchers are talking about (Giles, 2007).

Post-publication review is not new. In physics, researchers publish work themselves on the arXiv pre-print server, and it is on arXiv that physicists find new research. Traditional publication in journals still happens, but is not necessarily required in order to disseminate the work, just to get recognized credit.

Similar systems have been tried in the life sciences – by Nature Precedings and Genome Research's pre-prints area, both now defunct, and, more recently and most promisingly, the bioRxiv server (www.biorxiv.org) run by Cold Spring Harbour Laboratory Press – but haven't to date gained as much traction. Suggestions for why vary, from fear of being scooped to the fear that some life sciences journals will refuse to publish manuscripts previously submitted to a pre-print server (Desjardins-Proulx et al., 2013).

To return to *PLOS ONE*, it soon became clear that commenting directly on papers on the journal website wasn't as successful as had been hoped, but not because no commentary was happening; rather, it was happening elsewhere. As Chris Surridge, managing editor of *PLOS ONE* at the time, blogged:

> It is clear that commenting on a PLOS ONE paper, let alone annotating one, can be a daunting prospect if your comments are presented right alongside the paper itself. Readers want to think about what they are going to say rather than make off-the-cuff remarks. PLOS ONE papers aren't a blog entry where all activity will be pretty much over within a couple of days. PLOS ONE papers are part of the scientific record and will be read and commented on for years to come. . . .
>
> There is only a single comment made on [a recent paper]. What the comment does is point out to a posting about the paper on the Gene Expression blog. That posting has twenty five associated comments which form a really good discussion of the underlying evolutionary pressures which might favour this behaviour.
>
> (Surridge, 2007)

There were lots of possible reasons for this. As Surridge suggested, it might partly have been because users didn't feel comfortable about leaving their comment directly on the article itself, as it felt too permanent. PLOS eventually addressed the issue by adding trackbacks from blogs to its publishing platform in September 2007 and by pulling data from research blog aggregators like Postgenomic.com and ResearchBlogging.org soon thereafter.

The Faculty of 1000 (www.f1000.com), started in 2002, began by taking a different approach. Rather than providing a publishing and commenting platform it recruited 'faculty' – academics who were willing to contribute named, short reviews and ratings of papers published elsewhere to the F1000 database. The F1000 database recorded only 'good' papers – there is no rating for a paper that is misleading or wrong.

By setting up saved searches on the F1000 platform end-users can be alerted to papers that the F1000 faculty believe are of high quality or otherwise noteworthy.

Researcher blogs

Postgenomic.com, ResearchBlogging.org (both now defunct) and ScienceSeeker.org all aimed to collect posts from blogs written by researchers and/or that were concerned for the most part with discussing the scholarly literature. Other blog aggregators and search engines existed but didn't typically differentiate between 'researcher' blogs and other kinds of blogs, like those set up purely for spam or marketing purposes.

As *PLOS ONE* recognized early on, while researchers seem reluctant to comment on articles on journal platforms they do seem comfortable to do so on third-party blogs.

Blog posts about papers can range from simple lists of links – listing, for example, links that the blog's author has found interesting over the past week or two – to more in-depth mini-reviews of single papers or topics.

Interestingly, while post-publication review does happen on blogs, it is not necessarily something that the blogger has set out to do; rather, it can be a side-effect of the blogger's writing about the research that interests them. The motivations behind research blogging vary. Researchers' blogs are sometimes started because the blogger wants to talk about their own work, to engage in discussion or sometimes just because they enjoy writing (Mahrt and Puschmann, 2014).

While they do not constitute as high a volume as Mendeley readers or shares on social media sites like Facebook and Twitter, there are still a considerable number of researchers' blog posts about articles. Nicolás Robinson-García et al. found that, of approximately 450,000 articles in Web of Science published between 2011 and 2013 for which some altmetrics data was available, some 50,000 had been blogged about at least once (Robinson-García et al., 2014).

Wider changes in scholarly communications and its infrastructure
Moving away from journal-level metrics

It has been acknowledged that the impact factor, which reflects the average number of citations of recent articles in a journal, has gradually come to be misused as the primary 'shortcut' for comparing the output of individuals and institutions (Simons, 2008).

There are many problems with using the impact factor in this way, but the principal one is that citation distributions within journals are heavily skewed. A high-impact journal contains papers with almost no citations; conversely, low-impact journals contain papers that are cited very heavily. Furthermore, the impact factor itself is heavily influenced by the mix of article types and subjects represented in the journal; a high-impact factor for a physics journal may be considered low for a life sciences journal.

In 2013 a group of scientific societies, journals and institutions came together to sign DORA, the San Francisco Declaration on Research Assessment (www.ascb.org/dora/). DORA makes a number of different recommendations, but in essence calls on institutions, publishers and researchers to stop using journal-level metrics and instead focus on individual outputs – including datasets and software – and to consider a range of different indicators, both qualitative and quantitative, not just citations.

Importantly for altmetrics, DORA also contains recommendations for metrics providers: that the data they provide should be as open and transparent as possible, that they should commit to dealing with gaming, and that they should account for different article types and subject areas.

In January 2015 DORA had more than 12,000 individual and 547 organizational signatories, including societies like the American Association for the Advancement of Science and the European Molecular Biology Organization, and funders like the Wellcome Trust and the Austrian Science Fund.

DOIs, CrossRef and DataCite

On a more pragmatic note, one challenge faced by altmetrics is that while users typically link to a specific version of an article or other output – for example, the version of the article on the publisher's site – many other copies of the same article may exist: on pre-print servers, as author copies and on aggregators like institutional repositories or the National Center for Biotechnology Information's (NCBI's) PubMedCentral service. In theory, the altmetrics data for all of these different copies should be collated.

However, things move around on the web all the time and this means that links are easily broken. It's also difficult to tell when two resources on different websites are separate items or just different versions of the same resource.

For example, why is the abstract of an article on the publisher's site different from the abstract of the same article on PubMed? The answer actually lies in the context, but it is useful to be able to tie these items together logically and consistently. For this, we're able to use the DOI, or digital object identifier.

These are issued centrally by an issuing agency. The vast majority of academic publishers using DOIs get them from CrossRef (www.crossref.org), an industry body charged with maintaining the scholarly DOI infrastructure. CrossRef charges a small fee per DOI.

It's useful to know why CrossRef exists at all: when articles first started to appear on the web one obvious use was to link citations in the reference section of each article to the relevant pages at other publishers' sites. By this means a researcher could jump from one paper to the other, following interesting trails of evidence.

The immediate stumbling block is that there is no reliable, programmatic way to go from a bibliographic citation – with a title, author, journal name, page number and so on – to a web address.

One might imagine a pattern that publishers could agree on – perhaps the bibliographic information could be part of the URL. Indeed, a system like this, called OpenURL (Van de Sompel and Beit-Arie, 2001), is used widely in academic libraries. But what would resolve these URLs, given that an article may move from publisher to publisher when journals are closed or bought and transferred, and that web domains change relatively frequently? (For example, to access content from the *Journal of the American Medical Association* in 2011 you would have visited jama.org – in 2014 you visit jamanetwork.org.)

CrossRef was formed to be the cross-publisher agency to help solve this problem. It would issue DOIs, which member publishers promised always to resolve to the most recent version of the paper. It would also hold metadata centrally, so as to allow publishers to quickly look up DOIs from other publishers, given only bibliographic metadata. It takes its name from this use case – Cross (publisher) Ref(-erence lookup).

Other agencies, like the DataCite consortium run by the Californian Digital Library and British Library, also issue DOIs to institutional data repositories and professional dataset managers like figshare.

Collecting altmetrics data for articles is made immeasurably easier by DOIs and the journals and repositories that assign them.

Form follows function – how early tools shaped how altmetrics is used

While the Altmetrics Manifesto was shared and read by many librarians, publishers and others working in scholarly communication, the first time that most researchers, research administrators or funders hear about altmetrics is when they come face to face with one of the tools available.

There have been a number of altmetrics workshops and conferences bringing together industry and academia – usually tool and data providers together with bibliometricians and librarians – notably the altmetrics workshops at the ACM Web Science conferences, the article-level metrics workshops organized by PLOS, and 1:AM and 2:AM (the first and second Altmetrics Conferences), which bring together funders, research administrators and altmetrics groups in Europe.

At the time of writing in late 2015, these meetings were beginning to bear fruit in the form of use cases and systems being adapted to meet the actual (rather than predicted) needs of their end-users. NISO, the North American standards body, was organizing working groups of altmetrics users and other stakeholders to address issues of standardization and language.

In the meantime, standards and guides for how altmetrics should be used have come, for better or worse, from the tool providers themselves, based on their interactions with early adopters.

Many tool-provider staff – at Impactstory, PLOS and Altmetric.com – were already connected in some way to open science or the future of scholarly communications communities like Force 11 (www.force11. org). Impactstory and PLOS are also both explicitly not for profit. Elsevier, another important tool provider, while less 'open', brought a nuanced view of citations and how metrics are used at institutions to workshops and group discussions.

This is the background that has shaped early and generally shared guidelines for using altmetrics data. Specifically:

1 When a number is used as an indicator or metric the data behind it should be available to inspect somehow. The data should be *auditable*.
2 The data should be *as open as possible* – where 'open' can mean either transparently collected or free to view.
3 It should be *meaningful* – the data collected should be relevant to the needs of end-users – it's easy to collect hundreds of different data points, harder to guide users who need to then interpret them.

As institutions and funders continue to develop their own guidelines for the use of altmetrics data it's likely that new rules will appear and older ones will be adapted to suit practice rather than theory.

In some cases this is already happening. Third-party licensing restrictions make completely open data (in the 'free' sense of the word) difficult, from both a cost and a legal point of view. To keep the data auditable, providers have to make a choice between leaving out sources of data that are just numbers – like downloads on most platforms, or Facebook Likes – or including them but having their users trust that they are correct.

Key points

- The thinking behind altmetrics in general and the Altmetrics Manifesto in particular was informed and inspired by Web 2.0 concepts and ideas:
  - □ Filter failure suggested that filtering articles for quality could happen downstream from the journals that published them.
  - □ The wisdom of crowds suggested that information aggregated from a group of researchers might sometimes help readers to make decisions better than the ones they might otherwise have made.
  - □ Collaborative filtering showed how a 'composite trace' of online activity might be used to help power new filters for discovery.
  - □ Crowdsourcing suggested that tasks like peer review – once performed by only a few select reviewers picked by the journal – could be outsourced to a larger crowd.
- Altmetrics was made possible because of four larger forces at work:
  - □ scholarship moving online, opening the way for new tools to help discover, consume and produce research
  - □ researcher engagement with those tools, allowing activity to be tracked in a systematic, unbiased way
  - □ interest from funders in non-traditional research outputs and in finding evidence for the broader value of research to society
  - □ wider changes in scholarly communications, like the movement away from journal-level and towards article-level metrics, and enabling infrastructure like CrossRef.
- The original guidelines for how to use altmetrics data were set by altmetrics tool providers rather than by end-users, although this is now changing.

References

Desjardins-Proulx, P. et al. (2013) The Case for Open Preprints in Biology, *PLoS Biolog*, **11** (5), e1001563.

Dinsmore, A., Allen, L. and Dolby, K. (2014) Alternative Perspectives on Impact: the potential of ALMs and altmetrics to inform funders about research impact, *PLOS Biology*, **12** (11), e1002003.

Giles, J. (2007) Open-access Journal Will Publish First, Judge Later, *Nature*, **445** (9), 445009a.

Haplin, H., Robu, V. and Shepherd, H. (2007) The Complex Dynamics of

Collaborative Tagging. In *Proceedings of International Conference on World Wide Web 2007, The University of Calgary, Banff National Park.*

Hull, D., Pettifer, S. and Kell, D. (2008) Defrosting the Digital Library: bibliographic tools for the next generation web, *PLOS Computational Biology,* **4** (10), e1000204.

Mahrt, M. and Puschman, C. (2014) Science Blogging: an exploratory study of motives, styles, and audience reactions, *JCOM The Journal of Science Communication,* **13** (03), A05.

Priem, J., Taraborelli, D., Groth, P. and Neylon, C. (2010) *Altmetrics: a manifesto,* www.altmetrics.org/manifesto.

Robinson-García, N., Torres-Salinas, D., Zahedi, Z. and Costas, R. (2014) New Data, New Possibilities: exploring the insides of Altmetric.com, *El Profesional de la Informacion,* **23** (4), 359–66.

Safire, W. (2009) Fat Tail, *New York Times,* 5 February, www.nytimes.com/2009/02/08/magazine/08wwln-safire-t.html.

Shirky, C. (2009) *It's Not Information Overload. It's filter failure,* https://www.youtube.com/watch?v=LabqeJEOQyI#t=126.

Simons, K. (2008) The Misused Impact Factor, *Science,* **322** (3899), 165.

Surowiecki, J. (2004) *The Wisdom of Crowds,* Doubleday.

Surridge, C. (2007) *To Post or Not To Post,* http://blogs.plos.org/plos/2007/02/to-post-or-not-to-post/.

Van de Sompel, H. and Beit-Arie, O. (2001) Open Linking in the Scholarly Information Environment Using the OpenURL Framework, *New Review of Information Networking,* **7** (1), 59–76.

Ware, M. and Mabe, M. (2012) *The STM Report: an overview of scientific and scholarly journal publishing,* 3rd edn, STM: International Association of Scientific, Technical and Medical Publishers.

Further reading

For more on the collaborative use of online tools by scientists see Nielsen, M. (2011) *Reinventing Discovery,* Princeton University Press.

A detailed history of how the CrossRef initiative came about can be found in *The Formation of CrossRef: a short history,* www.crossref.org/08downloads/CrossRef10Years.pdf.

CHAPTER 6

Beyond bibliometrics: altmetrics reflects information about engagement with more types of scholarly content from more types of consumers

William Gunn

Introduction

This chapter will discuss how altmetrics conveys additional information about research impact that isn't captured by traditional metrics. The focus of the chapter will be the hybrid platform Mendeley, which helps researchers to manage references, discover research and form social connections with peers. The chapter will investigate the metrics relevant to this topic and how they can be understood by LIS professionals and academics. The characteristics of these metrics will be explored in detail. The particular focus is on Mendeley readership because that's where my expertise lies, but there are many sources of altmetrics that serve a range of needs.

Mendeley and librarians

Reference management has for a long time been an important application in the LIS professional's toolbox. Used primarily by academics as a way to organize and embed research literature and evidence into their work, it remained mostly undeveloped until the likes of Connotea, Mendeley and CiteULike appeared. Many academic librarians are adept at reference management, which goes hand in hand with literature searching. As part of their role they provide knowledge and expertise to researchers and students on how to use reference management packages. Reference management underpins the systematic and correct approach to research production. Tools have been developed ranging from the established platforms such as EndNote, Reference Manager and RefWorks to a newer, web-based generation of tools such as Mendeley and CiteULike. This second generation of reference management tools takes into account the need for sharing references, accessing them on the web and a social dimension. Tools such as Connotea, CiteULike, Zotero and Mendeley have brought about a shift in reference management. The tool that I will focus on in this chapter is Mendeley, which introduced an alternative metric that allows users to discover papers based on their readership. The purpose of the chapter is to explore some of the functionality and reasons behind some of these new possibilities, using Mendeley's model as a case study. The chapter will look at the different metrics and how they work alongside the other metrics and platforms covered in this book.

Authors

When people think about metrics applied to authorship, they probably first think of citations. A citation is one way to make reference to a scholarly work, by referring to it in another scholarly publication. However, citations are only one means of referring to just one kind of scholarly work such as a journal or book. Altmetrics seeks to broaden the definition of scholarly references beyond citations and impact scores, in addition to the broader sources in which those references may be found. The types of altmetrics relevant to an author are those that refer to their works. Primarily, these are the number of views, reads or downloads of the work, but they also include measures that look more at reuse than at consumption. Three major distinctions within author-centric metrics are coverage (what fraction of scholarly content is covered by the metric), specificity (what fraction of the counts are intentional acts by a researcher on an object relevant to them) and rate of accrual.

Page views

HTML page views occur when a reader visits a web page which contains the work we are wanting to measure. Page views are one of the more quickly accumulating metrics, but they are also fairly noisy, in that they are driven primarily by the rank of the link to the work on a search results page and the frequency with which the search query leading to the search results page is run. This means that often a large percentage of page views are by searchers who do not find what they're looking for on the page and quickly navigate away. This can give a false indicator of the importance of a page or of a work within that page. Common sources of noise come from the repurposing of terms by research fields, as with transcription and translation in molecular biology or the use of Greek characters for special purposes in biology, astrophysics, maths and linguistics.

All research published online has at least some level of page views, so the coverage of the literature by this metric is among the highest of all metrics. There remains some disciplinary skew in this metric, however, as many types of humanities outputs do not have a canonical representation on the web (performance-based work, primarily), and many historical artefacts remain to be digitized. Other sources of skew come from the relative numbers of searchers in various fields, with science and engineering also having significant second-order effects from the greater penetration of sites discussing STM (science, technology and medicine) content, such as Stack Exchange and Quora. Authors of work that is primarily of interest to those working on problems of interest to disadvantaged demographics will find fewer page views of their work, as their demographic has less access to computers. In addition, HTML page views have to be adjusted for visits arising from programmatic fetching of pages, such as those arising from the activity of search engines systematically indexing pages.

PDF downloads

Another type of altmetric relevant to an author is a PDF download. This occurs with less frequency than HTML page views, and is still driven primarily by search, but has significantly greater engagement. For example, many readers looking for information about the history of the Greek letter *tau* may land on a page about a research paper covering tau protein, but few would then go on to download the PDF. PDF downloads therefore have slightly less coverage, but are far less noisy and much more closely correlated with citation. PDF downloads also occur with nearly the same kinetics as page views, making them one of the best early indicators of impact. The primary drawback of the PDF download metric is that it applies only to published research papers, and not to other types of scholarly works. It is subject to the same types of disciplinary skew as page views, only to a greater degree. PDF downloads are also subject to inflation via automated downloads and search engine indexing, although not all automated access is simply for building search engines. Often, PDFs are automatically downloaded for scholarly purposes such as content mining, wherein assertions, images, tables etc. are extracted from a large corpus of documents and used to aid in hypothesis generation or used directly in computer science research on content mining.

XML downloads

XML, or Extensible Markup Language, is a document format wherein information about the document, such as publication details, formatting and structure, is represented within the document itself by the use of special formatting conventions called tags. This is the format underlying many publishing and typesetting systems and usually isn't presented to a reader. However, this format is ideal for automated retrieval and processing, as the XML tags enable flexible reformatting and granular analysis of the document. The coverage is therefore lower, but because of significant efforts in the library, archive, and museum world to build representations of their collections as Linked Open Data, it can be one of the better sources of metrics for a scholar who has produced a non-article work. This metric gives a more focused look at reuse, as the only reason to consume the XML would be for computation, not for reading. Publishers continue to make available greater access to XML as researcher demand for it grows. Notably, Elsevier has opened access to the XML of its journal articles for Science Direct subscribers, and the digital analysis of large corpora of texts is a rapidly growing field of study. The time course of XML downloads is generally slower than that of other metrics, reflecting the use of XML versions of works in computational analysis, but has a longer half-life.

In the future, as alternative reading interfaces such as eLife Lens become more popular, this metric will probably need to be broken down into use for mining and use via reading interfaces.

Usage metrics

There are many secondary uses of scholarly content that are significant sources of author-relevant metrics with various levels of pertinence based on field. The primary source of usage metrics comes from the addition of a reference to a reference management tool. This metric goes one step beyond viewing or downloading and indicates possible intent to cite the work. As can be seen from the improved correlation between readership and citations relative to page views or downloads, addition to a reference manager is a clearer indication of scholarly use, although there is a time lag between addition to a reference manager and citation of the work in a manuscript. I discuss Mendeley as a source of article-level metrics below. Usage metrics are subject to the same skew as PDF downloads, with additional skew created by varying adoption of tools across disciplines. Mendeley has seen greater adoption in the sciences, while Zotero has more use in the humanities. Currently, usage metrics mostly focus on articles, but coverage of non-PDF types of works will expand as Mendeley develops services to support management of data and software.

Examining item usage in order to determine impact is a very old practice. Libraries and publishers have been collecting and using usage-based metrics for a long time in the form of counter reports, interlibrary loan requests and other such indicators, so altmetrics doesn't claim to be novel in the application of usage metrics to the assessment of academic impact. Instead, it aims to add new types of usage and new objects of use, and to do this at web scale rather than locally to one institution. One of the more interesting forms of usage is what's reflected in scholars' use of social networks to discover and share academic material. This material comes in many forms, some heavy and content rich, such as blog posts or Wikipedia links, some plentiful yet content poor. On the plentiful side, Twitter has emerged as an important source of scholarly signals. While this is convenient because many scholars use Twitter, and tweets are public and can easily be gathered and analysed, the limited context available in a tweet provides an indication that the article cited may have been read, but little more. On the other side, blog posts and Wikipedia entries provide a very strong signal that a work is useful to scholars, but the relative amount of literature that appears in a blog post is fairly small, limiting its systematic use. The happy middle ground is occupied by social bookmarking tools and academic reference managers. These tools have broad enough adoption by scholars to have reasonably good coverage of the literature, and the presence of a document in a reference manager is a much clearer signal that the article is influencing research. Mendeley is one of those tools and provides plenty of context via metadata capture and user profiles, opening up the possibility of filtering the social signals; other social platforms such as PubChase, Sparrho, MyScienceWork, ResearchGate and Academia.edu make available their own metrics reflecting how users engage with their sites. It is important to note that differences in how the various communities use the available tools modify how impact is reflected by the tool, and in addition the newness of many of these tools biases them to more recent literature. Thus, it's worth discussing Mendeley as a source of metrics, and what types of impact are reflected in the data available from the platform.

What data does Mendeley collect?

Mendeley is a reference management tool for researchers to organize, share and discover research. It has broad adoption across disciplines, with around the largest number of researchers being in life sciences, chemistry, maths and computer science, but also with representation from the social sciences and non-journal-based humanities disciplines. Accordingly, the research catalogue has the best coverage in the sciences, often having greater than 90% coverage of recent issues of many journals. The greater representation of the sciences in Mendeley is thought to be primarily a reflection of its PDF-centric workflow and the journal-article-centric communication in the sciences.

Researchers use Mendeley to store research papers and other publications along with the metadata about those publications, to share those papers or collections of papers with colleagues, and to discover new material based on what others are reading. The activity on Mendeley therefore provides many signals that reflect different types of impact, and there have been numerous studies comparing how many people have an item in their Mendeley library with citations, impact factor, F1000, article downloads and social bookmarking.

Mendeley can return quite a lot of aggregated, anonymous data about the usage of a publication found in its index. Figure 6.1 is an example of the data returned from a document details call to Mendeley. Note that some documents with low representation in the Mendeley catalogue may not be available via the Application Program Interface (API), because of content-quality filter-suppressing of results for these documents. As Mendeley refines the crowdsourced data with the 'ground truth' data from Scopus, this restriction will be removed.

Discussion of a few of the items returned by a details call and what they, individually and in the aggregate, can tell us about scholarly activity is in order.

Keywords

Keywords are user-generated content that provide an indication of what the author thinks are significant concepts or relationships in the paper. Mendeley currently returns only the author-supplied keywords in response to a request for the public details for a paper. Any tags that an individual user has added can be retrieved only by permission of the user by a separate, user-specific call for the document details.

Identifiers

Identifiers are the other names by which the document is known. These may be a PubMed ID, an arXiv ID, a DOI or an ISSN. Included elsewhere in the document details data are a UUID (Universal Unique Identifier) for the document and an article page URL and page slug. These identifiers are useful for querying other databases about documents found at Mendeley in order to find out what data the other database may have, or as a shorthand way of making subsequent calls to the Mendeley API for a given document.

```
{"abstract":"Diabetic complication is comprised of
[truncated]",
"keywords":[
        Interleukin 18",
        "diabetic nephropathy",
        "high sensitive CRP",
        "proinflammatory cytokine",
        "oxidative stress",
        "adipokine"],
"website":"http:\/\/www.ncbi.nlm.nih.gov\/pubmed\/20186552",
"identifiers":{
        "pmid":"20186552",
        "issn":"14325233",
        "doi":"10.1007\/s00592-010-0178-4"},
"stats":{
        "readers":7,
        "discipline":[
                {"id":3,"name":"Biological
Sciences","value":71},
                {"id":19,"name":"Medicine","value":29}],
        "country":[
                {"name":"United States","value":29},
                {"name":"Brazil","value":29},
                {"name":"United Kingdom","value":14}],
        "status":[
                {"name":"Doctoral Student","value":29},
                {"name":"Student (Master)","value":14},
                {"name":"Post Doc","value":14}]},
"issue":"2",
"pages":"111-7",
"publication_outlet":"Acta Diabetologica",
"type":"Journal Article",
"url":"interleukin-18-contributes-more-closely-progression-
diabetic-nephropathy-other-diabetic-complication",
"uuid":"8af2c880-cd0d-11df-922b-0024e8453de6",
"authors":[
        {"forename":"Takayuki","surname":"Fujita"},
        {"forename":"Norikazu","surname":"Ogihara"},
        {"forename":"Yumi","surname":"Kamura"},
        {"forename":"Atsushi","surname":"Satomura"},
        {"forename":"Yoshinobu","surname":"Fuke"},
```

Figure 6.1 *Example of the data returned from a document details call to Mendeley (continued on next page)*

```
        { "forename":"Chie","surname":"Shimizu"},
        { "forename":"Yuki","surname":"Wada"},
        { "forename":"Koichi","surname":"Matsumoto"}
],
"title":"Interleukin-18 contributes more closely to the
progression of diabetic nephropathy than other diabetic
complications.",
"volume":"49",
"year":2010,
"categories":[ 338,43],
"oa_journal":false,
"mendeley_url":"http:\/\/api.mendeley.com\/research\/interleuk
in-18-contributes-more-closely-progression-diabetic-
nephropathy-other-diabetic-complication\/"}
```

Figure 6.1 *(continued)*

Stats

The Stats array in Mendeley contains several data structures which contain descriptive information about the document:

- *Readers*. This is the number of Mendeley users who have a given document in their library. This number includes all copies of a document, including citation-only entries, and is updated approximately daily. This value is perhaps one of the most interesting from an altmetrics point of view, and more details about how this number is derived can be found in the following section on readers. The number is broken down below, but note that in all cases only aggregate numbers are presented and individual users are not identified.
- *Discipline*. This is the breakdown of the disciplines of the readers, given as whole-number percentages of the total readership. The discipline name, ID and percentage are given for the top three disciplines. You can use this information to get a picture of the relative impact of a document in a specific field. For example, in Figure 6.1, five (value 71) of the readers come from biological sciences, and two (value 29) from medicine. Because the numbers add up to 100%, there are no readers from other disciplines reading this document. At the moment, a reader may have only one discipline, which they select at signup, and all their reading is attributed to that discipline. At the

time of writing this chapter Mendeley plans to transition to a flexible tag-based system for discipline assignment.

- *Country*. This reports data about the geographic dispersal of readers, reported as percentages, as shown Figure 6.1. You can use this data to plot the impact of a work or set of works on a map at the country level. More granular readership information is coming, but because of privacy issues there are no plans to report city-level data.
- *Status*. This reports data on the readership by academic discipline, which can be selected at signup. One way to use this data is to determine if research is having more of an impact on early-stage researchers relative to senior investigators, but there are classifications for non-research professions as well, which allows practitioner versus researcher analyses.

Categories

Categories are given as numerical IDs and map onto the disciplines and sub-disciplines that Mendeley users assign to themselves.

URLs and UUIDs

URLs and UUIDs give the value of the unique identifier of the document in Mendeley, as well as the page slug for the article. So if you had a PubMed identifier (PMID) and wanted to find the page on Mendeley for the article you would first carry out a details call, pasting in the PMID, and then append the value of the URL to www.mendeley.com/catalog/ to get the article's page URL.

Mendeley readership

The number of readers of a document on Mendeley is one of the potentially most interesting numbers from an altmetrics point of view. This number reflects the number of Mendeley users who have the document in their library. On a lower level, this number is the size of a document cluster. The Mendeley catalogue is generated by a clustering algorithm which runs approximately daily across the entirety of the Mendeley catalogue, processing about a half a billion documents a day and clustering duplicates of the same document into one canonical representation. The size of this cluster is the readership of the document it contains. Occasionally, when the catalogue is regenerated, multiple clusters are generated for the same document. This happens primarily with documents that have been uploaded hundreds of times in various forms and with various modifications made to their metadata by users. If there's duplication, the number of clusters is usually around three to five, with readers distributed randomly among them. This cluster instability is the reason why numbers for a given document sometimes seem to go down, and the remedy is to track and combine the various duplicates of the document until they all collapse into one. When Mendeley builds a 'ground truth' set of metadata into the catalogue via Scopus, documents are assigned to a permanent cluster, thus eliminating cluster instability.

How does Mendeley readership compare with other metrics, such as citations or article downloads?

There are a few things to keep in mind when considering the meaning of Mendeley readership or any other altmetric. The first thing to remember is that Twitter has been around only since 2006, and Mendeley since 2008, and, given that papers accrue most of their citations in the first six to twelve months, it's reasonable to expect altmetrics to favour recent papers as well. It's also important to keep the different citation practices of various fields in mind when comparing quantitative metrics to citations. When we look at Mendeley's data and traditional citations there is a within-field correlation between readers and papers, but when we look at multidisciplinary non-open-access publications such as *Cell*, *Nature* and *Science*, the relationship appears much weaker. It is interesting to note that open access papers enjoy a significant advantage relative to non-open-access papers, having double the number of Mendeley readers.

Non-author uses of metrics

The above descriptions of alternative metrics sources are somewhat author- and paper-centric. However, since the focus of altmetrics is, by design, broader than authors, there are many impacts on other stakeholders in research, such as publishers, funders, librarians, policymakers and the public. Importantly, the metrics are often the same, but the uses to which they are put are different.

Publishers use altmetrics to provide some of the author- and reader-centric metrics, but they also use it to promote site engagement via recommended and related articles. Funding agencies use it for tracking the return on investment of the research they fund. In a somewhat similar fashion, librarians and research administrators use it to track the impact of content in an institutional repository or to assess their department's strengths. The increasing use of altmetrics by funding organizations, publishers and tenure and promotion committees shows that there is broad awareness of the limitations of traditional citation-based metrics and a need to move beyond the paper-based mindset so as to take advantage of the more diverse forms of communication enabled by the internet.

One of the most novel and interesting kinds of impact revealed by the aggregation of online metrics of engagement is the impact on historically underrepresented stakeholders such as clinicians, patients and the public. These are the people outside the ivory tower. Engaging with these groups has traditionally been the realm of the media, including university press offices and popular science reporting. As such, what we know about what the public is interested in is filtered through the lens of media priorities. With altmetrics collected directly from individual members of the public, it becomes clearer where and to what extent the public is engaging with research, particularly within patient communities. The extent to which the research is connecting with the public can be seen directly from the latter's activity, providing funders and researchers with the ability to see directly the impact of their research, unmediated, and make the best case possible for the value of what they do.

To broaden the scope of the discussion beyond papers, let's consider different kinds of reuse of scholarly works and the impacts that they have. The ways in which research can be reused can be divided into five general categories based on application: inspiring new research; mining existing data for novel associations; application or implementation; contribution to popular understanding; and meta-analysis. The various types of reuse and how these can be tracked for discovery and assessment, briefly discussed below, will be the subject of a forthcoming (US) National Information Standards Organization (NISO) white paper.

The first kind of reuse, inspiring new research, is well covered by the traditional databases that track citations, but is limited in that a subsequent piece of research points to a prior piece but the prior piece does not reciprocally point back to the subsequent research that it inspired. This type of reuse is inhibited through lack of access to the research. Additionally, the pointer is at the document level, which gives poor resolution of the details of the reuse. Another needed improvement for understanding citation behaviour is to enrich a citation by adding distinguishing characteristics that would allow the different types of citations to be distinguished from one another. See the Citation Typing Ontology (CiTO) for current work in this area.

Tracking mining of datasets, the second category of reuse, is often done by tracking the papers that describe them. However, more datasets are appearing on sites such as figshare and Dryad, which assign DOIs to the data directly, rather than just to a paper describing the data. Creating URIs (Uniform Resource Identifiers) that point to the data directly promotes the data to equal standing with a research paper because the data can now be referenced directly and accrue reuse separately from the paper. As with citation of papers, access to data is a barrier to reuse, and technical skills and equipment to handle the data are also needed.

When you move out of the scholarly realm and into applications, there are fewer explicit mentions of the original works themselves. A reuse event in a commercial application can be detected via looking for references in patent applications or publications arising from academic–industry collaborations, but this shows only first-order impact, at best, and as you move further away from the publication and into the inventions or policies that it may have enabled or informed the trail becomes very difficult to follow, even as the raw number of possible reuse events grows. This is where individual efforts such as the implementation of a Becker Model analysis become necessary, though this is prohibitive to do at scale.

Looking at the reuse of a scholarly work by the public is done much as with an application or implementation. The main source of reuse events in this category is mentions in popular media, although there is a significant 'long tail' of lay communities online that discuss research: patient communities, space aficionados, citizen scientists and teachers in non-professorial roles. Interestingly, PubMed Central reports that the majority of the page views to research papers hosted there come from non-institutional domains. Another notable feature of reuse within the public domain is that the direction of flow is reversed: external events such as natural disasters, celebrity endorsements or other news events often drive increased public reuse events, whereas the availability of a technology facilitates the application.

Meta-analysis is its own category of reuse. There's a growing movement to conduct and publish replication studies of existing work, such as the Reproducibility Initiative and the Reproducibility Project: Cancer Biology, a partnership between the Reproducibility Initiative and the Center for Open Science. The aims of these projects are to understand and promote replication of research as a type of reuse. The replication studies contain pointers to the original research and explicitly identify which experiments were carried out and what the results were. This enables the creation of a separate discovery layer, to highlight and identify the more reproducible or the most reusable work, facilitating downstream commercial application or reduction to practice.

Conclusion

Reference management is into a second era and is more important than it ever was. Researchers have not only a greater number of conventional research outputs to filter, such as journal papers, but also an increasingly wide array of grey literature, datasets and web artefacts, among other things, to manage. It seems natural that altmetrics should accompany such developments in a world where research is carried out globally across the web. Technologies such as Mendeley have set out to bridge the gap between function and discovery and are part of a much bigger mechanism. LIS professionals involved in research, from student support to research management, can benefit from understanding the different forms of metrics. These range from the traditional metrics of citations as covered in the earlier chapters of this book, to web metrics in this chapter, to altmetrics in the later chapters. As for altmetric tools, it is hoped that this chapter's focus on one particular tool and its use of metrics has given readers the widest possible vista of the myriad of metrics we can explore. Metrics give us a better idea of document reuse and scholarly communication, especially as the amount of research published grows, therefore making the case for reference management more strongly than ever.

Key points

- Reference management tools give us a new insight on research reuse.
- Tools such as Mendeley can give researchers a quick feedback loop to traditional citations that are slow to accrue.
- In between traditional citations and altmetrics there are other sets of metrics that can be applied to research, such as downloads, page views and reference management saves.
- Open access research enjoys a far greater readership in Mendeley than does research behind paywalls.
- Altmetrics offers many opportunities to those outside academic institutions, such as the 'long tail' of communities that discuss research.

Web resources

Citation Styles.org: http://citationstyles.org/.
CiTO The Citation Typing Ontology:
    www.essepuntato.it/lode/http://purl.org/spar/cito.
Mendeley.com: https://www.mendeley.com/.
Mendeley Help Guides: https://community.mendeley.com/guides.
Mendeley Research Blog: http://blog.mendeley.com/.

Further reading

Moore, S. A. (ed.) (2014) *Issues in Open Research Data,* Ubiquity Press.
Neal, D. (ed.) (2012) *Social Media for Academics: a practical guide,* Chandos Publishing.
Raubenheimer, J. (2014) *Mendeley: crowd-sourced reference and citation management in the information era,* Bloemfontein, True Insight Publishing.

CHAPTER 7

Considerations for implementing new technologies

Andy Tattersall

Introduction

This chapter aims to explain the various issues that need to be considered by researchers when applying new technologies, or by LIS professionals when encouraging researchers to take them up. The growing number of technologies, web, desktop or mobile, adds to the issues relating to their use. The chapter will investigate these issues, which academics and support professionals alike frequently fail to identify. Its pragmatic advice to readers is that, by following a few simple rules, these technologies can be applied with a minimum of fuss for a maximum of impact.

Teachers have a pedagogy; what do researchers employ?

Anyone who is directly involved in any kind of technology-enhanced teaching and support will seek to make good use of the available technologies and will have to make informed judgements as to whether a specific technology will a make useful contribution to their task. Such decisions are led by the pedagogy, that is, the practice of how best to teach. A competent teacher or learning technologist will endeavour to use a technology to enhance their or the lecturer's teaching and the students' learning experience. By just using technology for its own sake, teachers run the risk of disrupting the learning process and negatively affecting the classroom and its learning objectives. The same can be said in research, because altmetrics and other social and web technologies can be regarded as disrupters. The impact of MOOCs on learning, open access on publishing and big data on research data all show that there are changes afoot within the academic community. These innovations have come to us through technology and have disrupted higher education and research in varying degrees. In the longer term, it would be good to be able to look back and see them as changes for the good, but it is too early to judge just yet. Certainly, many academics would agree that the existing systems of delivering lectures, managing and publishing research needed to be overhauled for the 21st century. So, as the hardware and software become more readily available, it makes sense to explore the possibilities that they present.

Plenty of academics are already making good use of altmetrics and the wealth of scholarly communication tools that are now available. Some will have done so as a natural progression, as part of their professional development and out of a natural interest in technology and the web; others will have made a simple leap of faith; and some, no doubt, will have been coerced against their will. What we are seeing is just the tip of the iceberg. The bulk of the academic community has yet to get online in truly meaningful ways that go beyond the creation of a social media profile and updating a few papers. The majority of academics, at both ends of the age spectrum, need a mix of ideas and support systems to help them engage more with the web. Of course, not all of them will want to do so, and until there are formal initiatives for change it is unlikely that we will see the levels of technology and web use in academia that are found elsewhere in society. Also given that it is over a decade since the term Web 2.0 was popularized as a concept in 2005, it could be at least another decade before we see a genuinely widespread uptake of these technologies. There are various reasons why academics do not engage with technology as a means of driving change in the way that some other professionals do. The majority of academics who are not engaging with social media and altmetrics may have good reasons, but the technologies are not going to go away and many of those who do take advantage of them will claim that they have benefited from doing so. These benefits include invitations to write, to present their work, to collaborate and to discover knowledge that is useful to them and their work. Every researcher will have their own story, big or small. It is important for the majority who are not yet using these technologies to hear about them via case studies and to make informed decisions about whether or not to join in.

In terms of the research community's take-up of these technologies, there is a need for the equivalent of a pedagogy. There is also a need for support systems and champions, so that even if a researcher decides that they do not wish to use the new technologies to share, communicate or measure their research, they will at least have explored the evidence available to them.

What makes a good tool?

Before we look at specific technologies in the next chapter, it is important to discuss briefly what qualities make for a good piece of technology. This is especially relevant when a variety of similar technologies are competing for your attention.

Communication

This may seem like a less obvious aspect of what makes a good technology, but in the age of social media, communication with technology users is important. For example, does the technology have a Twitter feed? If the provider's website goes offline, you will be able to check their Twitter feed for status updates. Can you find out about latest developments, and whether a new version of the software is on the horizon? What will the changes be and what impact might they have on researchers in your organization who are using the technology?

User engagement

On another aspect of communication, is there a two-way conversation between the technology provider and users? For example, does the provider ask users for input on such matters as feature requests and bug fixes? An excellent example of this is Mendeley, which has set up a Mendeley Advisor scheme to encourage early adopters to provide feedback and suggest new functions via discussion lists, voting systems and open days. Globally, there are now over 1000 Mendeley Advisors, many of whom communicate with the company on a regular basis. Despite Mendeley's increase in size and subsequent takeover by publishing giant Elsevier, this model remains an important part of Mendeley's development process.

Export functionality

One of the worst things that can happen to anyone who puts their trust in a technology is that it ceases to exist and all their data and content is lost. In most cases users receive advance warning; in other cases, users' 'gut feeling' and social networks enable them to deduce that a key person is no longer at the helm of a website or tool. This is more often the case for small tools or technologies that have been set up by one or two people – in the case of academic tools, as the result of a research project. It is therefore important to investigate whether the technology in question has an export function. Even giants such as Google can create a huge stir when they close or mothball a tool, the best example being that of the superb RSS aggregator Google Reader. It was used by millions, including many in the academic community, to stay up to date with the latest published research, but was closed because Google wanted to focus on other areas of content curation. Google gave its Reader users several months to find another aggregator, and the majority left for the even more popular tool Feedly. Another example is iGoogle, a personalized portal home page that was discontinued in 2013, despite its having a loyal and extensive user base. It came complete with Google search function, and users could add their diaries, news feeds and local weather to a single home page.

Who is behind the technology?

Even though a rule of thumb can be applied that the bigger the provider, the more likely that the technology will last, this is not always the case, as demonstrated by the above example of Google Reader. But for the most part this rule of thumb does offer some comfort to users of the technology. At the other end of the spectrum, technologies that are started as small research projects are much riskier for user, but they can go on to big things if another, bigger technology company buys them out, as happened in the case of Mendeley when it was taken over by Elsevier. Many altmetrics and scholarly communication tools are backed by large publishers, such as ReadCube by Macmillan Publishing and Connotea (now defunct) by Nature Publishing. The smaller technology start-ups, some of which began life as student and research projects, often have just one or two people working on them, and depending on the company's aspirations and resources it can take a while for them to become viable entities. When the dot.com bubble burst in the early 2000s many major websites lost value and some even stopped trading, and with many research-related start-ups there is always a fear that this could happen again. Not every academic-focused website will have solid financial backing, and in an increasingly competitive market some will fall by the wayside. Hence it is important to understand the factors that make a technology viable to use. However, in the author's experience the number of useful tools that have disappeared is small. Notable mentions include Pageflakes, Droiderly, Google Reader and Connotea, the latter to some extent being replaced by ReadCube.

Helping to translate the technology

Readers are likely to have heard of and used some of the technologies and websites mentioned in this book. Everyone has heard of Facebook, but this highly influential social networking tool is just one small part of altmetrics. The wealth of tools that are covered in this book can be viewed as the small cogs in a much larger, organic machine. Some are grouped together and work collaboratively, while others work more in isolation. It can feel daunting to discover a wealth of available tools when you are trying to understand an existing set of core technologies, such as library and teaching systems. Add to that the problem of translating these technologies to the researchers in our organization. This in itself is a difficult task, as researchers often struggle to find spare time. Gaining and holding their attention requires much hard work, and it is important to find new ways of capturing their attention. One good way is through video, which has become an essential element of communication on the web. I have created a series of short videos to help researchers and LIS professionals to quickly gain an understanding of some of the tools and ideas featured in this book. They are called Research Hacks and most of them run for fewer than two minutes. They provide an easy-to-understand explanation of tools such as figshare, Altmetric.com and Impactstory. They do not to go deeply into the technologies, but were created purely to spark curiosity and encourage users to explore the tools for themselves. In fact they could be regarded as a no-pressure sales pitch for technologies to aid scholarly productivity, communication and collaboration. The series of 45 short videos can be viewed at https://itunes.apple.com/gb/itunes-u/scharr-research-hacks/id985562918?mt=10.

Some words of caution

Before we move on to the next chapter, which looks at some of the many technologies and websites, you need to be aware of a few issues relating to them. Some are what are called third-party technologies and may offer little by way of redress or support should they stop a service, lose your data or share it with others outside your control. However, many of the tools covered in this book are provided by established, profit-making, mature companies that have a lot to offer to researchers and LIS professionals who want to use them. Here are a few things that you need to consider before using these technologies.

Does your institution offer an in-house alternative?

Any kind of content that you put on the web is at risk of disappearing or being stolen or misused. It is advisable to find a web or technology company that provides a service level agreement and assurance that your content will be available online 100% of the time, without interruption. It is important to consider what other options are available with regard to security and uninterrupted access, for instance whether your institution has a repository for publications, or a means of hosting digital content. However, in-house technologies can rarely match those available in the commercial sector, as the providers are invariably focusing on their product and supporting a larger customer base, whereas your own IT department has to support dozens of products for a smaller user base.

What are they doing with your data?

Since the mid-2000s we have become increasingly comfortable with sharing our personal data, whether that be baby photos, our geographical locations or our relationships – all of which help to feed data-hungry organizations such as Facebook and Google. However, it is difficult to find someone who has actually read the terms and conditions of the websites or apps that they sign up to. But it is important to consider, when using a new technology, who is behind it, what their purpose is and what they will do with your content. It is increasingly common for technology providers to encourage users to sign up via a more established technology such as Twitter, Google or Facebook. This is because many providers understand that there is a limit to the number of technologies a user will sign up to with unique credentials, and allowing users to sign up via an existing account removes this barrier. This can be done by using OAuth (open authorization), which allows users to access a resource via another resource (such as Twitter or Facebook) that they already have access to, without sharing their credentials. You may not stop to read the terms and conditions, but when you use any tools via OAuth it is important to be aware of what you are allowing one technology to do by interacting with another.

Can you put your content on the web?

Given that academic institutions are often quite liberal in sharing knowledge and expertise, it makes sense to encourage researchers to share content as far as possible across the web. However, some research is conducted on behalf of private organizations; publications can have embargoes; and most teaching materials are for the explicit use of specific degree-level courses. Thus, some academics may not be able to take advantage of such tools, for a variety of business-case reasons. Therefore it is important to understand what can be shared, whether that be a dataset, a pre-publication paper or a report.

Is your content copyright compliant?

Copyright can often be a grey area. The law is not always very clear, and this is especially so in education. A researcher may feel frustrated when an eagle-eyed support librarian warns them about copyright issues. Receiving contradictory advice as to what they can and cannot use may also be a problem. Often researchers are not inclined to tangle with the finer points of online copyright, and this becomes apparent when they start populating the web with their own presentations and content. The result can be that they stick to the tried and tested methods of bullet-pointed, text-heavy slides, rather than risk breaching copyright by incorporating images. Yet there are alternatives for researchers trying to move away from traditional presentations to a more attractive style, though it is important to note that this can also have a negative effect, as image-based presentations can sometimes make little sense if they are hosted online after a presentation. The same can be said about text only presentations, of course. Nevertheless there are benefits from putting presentations online in an attempt to make a researcher's work more visible. Recording the presentation provides additional context and more meaning to the slides. It is of course important for researchers and LIS professionals to explore the legal aspects of putting images online. Guidance on this point, and images that are not restricted by copyright, can be found on the Creative Commons website (https://creativecommons.org). Other options are to use an institutional asset bank of images or to take and use one's own photographs.

Are your opinions really yours?

Twitter is one the many social media areas where there can be a blur between professional and personal use. Some LIS professionals and academics choose to have separate accounts for professional and personal use; others focus purely on professional use, while many mix the personal and the professional. Users frequently apply caveats to their profile along the lines of 'views expressed here are my own'. Even so, if your profile is in some way linked to your institution, then your organization will take notice if some of your content is considered to be unprofessional. Researchers are not immune to the risk of posting tweets that are considered controversial or insulting.

Can you show someone how to use social media?

This is a frequent question. The internet has an underlying democratized ethos and it is said that people should be allowed to explore the web for themselves and use it as they wish. There may be guides on how to use the web, but you will still come across ethical issues with regard to a communication or something you have read that you have to deal with on your own initiative. It is important for any researchers whom you encourage to use social media and altmetrics to have a positive early experience that will help to skill them up for later on.

Conclusion

Researchers may already be accustomed to using social media on a personal level, posting holiday photos, discussing politics and the weather and sharing personal stories. Some may have an understanding of the privacy issues relating to social networks, while others will share content totally unaware of such implications. In an academic context, problems may arise for both the researcher and the institution when boundaries become blurred and the personal slips into the professional. LIS and other related professionals, such as learning technologists, communication specialists and administrators, can help to guide users toward good practice. This requires the professionals to have a good level of knowledge and to have explored the technologies and their issues. Books such as this one and others listed throughout it will supplement that knowledge.

Key points

- Researchers need support in adapting their use of social media and other technologies from a personal setting to a professional one.
- LIS professionals have the right skills to support both their peers and researchers in discovering and learning how to use new technologies.
- Digital copyright and literacy issues can be addressed by the library community both on campus and on the web.
- This is a fast-changing area within academia. New roles will be developed related to digital research and support that will create new opportunities for career progression within the library community.

■ LIS professionals can maximize their involvement and impact by making strong connections with the IT, learning technology and communication communities on campus.

Further reading

Carrigan, M. (2016) *Social Media for Academics*, Sage Publications.

Garoralo, D. (2013) *Building Communities*, Chandos.

Hoffman, S. (ed.) (2016) *Dynamic Research Support for Academic Libraries*, Facet Publishing.

O'Connor, S. (ed.) (2015) *Library Management in Disruptive Times: skills and knowledge for an uncertain future*, Facet Publishing.

Rowley, J. (2010) *Being an Information Innovator*, Facet Publishing.

Veletsianos, G. (2016) *Social Media in Academia*, Taylor & Francis.

CHAPTER 8

Resources and tools

Andy Tattersall

Introduction

This chapter will guide readers through the myriad of tools and resources that are available to help promote, share and measure scholarly output. It describes the catalogue of tools and techniques that LIS professionals can use themselves or teach to academics and their support staff to help them get their research out into the world. The tools and technologies can be divided into a number of categories, including academic networking, audio and visual technologies, content hosting and tools for measurement. Within these categories the tools are listed in alphabetical order. The list is by no means exhaustive, but looks at the key tools and discusses how some of them can be used.

One of the biggest difficulties in writing a chapter such as this is deciding which technologies and platforms to include. Technology is moving rapidly. This applies equally to altmetrics and scholarly communications, and by the time this book is published there will be even more tools and resources available. While the book's theme is altmetrics and the core altmetric tools, i.e. those that collate, measure and report scholarly and other forms of communication, this chapter also looks at the many other tools available for the communication of research. Some tools may be of use to those working in the sciences, others more applicable to medicine, and there will be much cross-over. There will be tools that you have already read about and used, but plenty of new ones to discover. While this book sets out to identify new ways of using some of these technologies, readers will, no doubt, come up with many others.

An introduction to scholarly communication and measurement tools

There are several useful ways to stay up to date with the discussion and developments around altmetrics, and these are listed in the web resources list at the end of this chapter. The chapter also looks at the implications of using some of these tools and the ethics and issues that LIS professionals and academics face in choosing where to invest their time and energy. The growing number of technologies creates an increasing number of choices; while some academics will successfully navigate their way through the available technologies for measuring and disseminating their work, others may find themselves lost in the ocean. The risk is that if academics have bad or unrewarding initial experiences with altmetric and scholarly communications tools, they may be reluctant to invest further time in these ways of working.

Among the large number of tools that can be used to share and measure academic content some are more important than others. Before investing time and other resources to discover, set up and manage any of these tools it is essential to have a good understanding of what a tool does and where and how it can be applied. Academics have constraints on their time and often need evidence for why they should change their ways of working. Guiding them towards tools that have clear and readily identifiable benefits is therefore a must. To some extent, discovering and investing time, energy and money in new technologies and ways of working is like stockbroking – one has to carefully pick the technologies to invest in, and the ones that will reap the biggest rewards.

Many of the platforms listed below are illustrated by animated video in my Research Hack series. There is inevitably some overlap between topics, and some tools may fit under several categories. For example, a tool like Mendeley can be considered a reference management tool, a database, a social network and an altmetrics platform.

It is impossible in the space available in this book to cover many of the tools in any real depth. For the majority, the focus is on the tool's key strengths. There are pointers to tools that you may already be aware of but for which you may not have recognized the connection to altmetrics. And while some of the tools may not qualify as altmetrics tools they nonetheless deserve mention under the umbrella of scholarly communication. During the research for this chapter it has become evident that many of the new generation of scholarly communication websites are very good at explaining what they do and how they work.

Building academic networks

This section focuses on the many academic and professional networks that exist and the reasons for joining them. It covers tools such as Twitter, Academia.edu, Mendeley, LinkedIn, ResearchGate and Google+, to name but a few. The number of social networks has grown rapidly since 2008, while user numbers have increased from the hundreds of thousands to millions and, in the case of Facebook, to over one billion. This growth has led to the development of niche networks that focus on hobbies and interests, geographical location, gender, religion and – for the focus of this book – academic networks.

Networking plays a large part in academia, whether through conferences, seminars, workshops, meetings or, more recently, techno-logical innovations such as webinars and teleconferences. A large part of what LIS professionals and academics do is underpinned by their ability to communicate, share and network. The growth of commercial and academic social networks has facilitated this, such that conversations no longer have to end at the close of a conference or when a project is completed. Compared to many of the other tools, social networks deserve greater consideration by academics over the long term.

Social networks
About.me

One problem for some researchers is that they have multiple social network profiles but no way to tie them together. They may not have their own website or blog and, if they are casual or honorary academics, may not even have their own staff page. Researchers who move jobs regularly also face the problem that building a consistent online CV with links becomes increasingly difficult. About.me is an aggregator of online presences that allows for a one-page text profile and photo. Despite being a far from comprehensive tool in terms of what it links to, you can connect from it to a few tools, including Twitter, LinkedIn, Facebook, Blogger and Google+. You can also add all of your contact details and links to your Mendeley profile, and even apply various keywords to describe your area of expertise.

Academia.edu

Academia.edu, together with ResearchGate, is one of the bigger, more established social networks for researchers. Its primary purpose is to encourage researchers from around the world to network and share papers. With over 20 million users and nearly 6 million papers, it is a huge database that allows users to read and share each other's research and provides analytics based on views and downloads of these papers.

Facebook

Facebook is used by many academics, not just on a personal level but also professionally. Mark Zuckerberg's social network provides possibly the greatest angst and concern for any LIS professional and academic when it is used on a professional level, and that extends to altmetrics. Facebook is more often than not seen as a personal social network and its use is regarded by many in the workplace as a distraction and not work. This is understandable when, in an age of digital distraction and decreasing attention spans, Facebook operates at the level of the subconscious of many of its users. The updates that happen by the second can be a constant lure for anyone who is not entirely interested in their work. Facebook has been criticized over its privacy settings and the risks posed to users following a change its privacy terms.

The issues posed by Facebook can put academics off using other social networking tools to share their ideas and knowledge, especially if they are not too sure about whom they are sharing it with. The LIS professional can help to allay such concerns by having a good understanding of the privacy and ethical issues. Facebook is the world's biggest online social network, and it is likely that even if you do not use Facebook, you will know someone who does. It allows its users to share their thoughts, links, photos and videos, amongst other things. Users can form private or public groups and can filter the posts from other users (known as friends) from the timeline to which they subscribe.

How Facebook can be applied

Many journals, blog posts and other web artefacts now have Facebook Likes on their pages to allow users to share or 'like' the content they read. This has value for users who create public posts that are monitored by tools such as Altmetric.com and that can be viewed for a specific journal or web article on the Altmetric.com dashboard.

Google+

Google+ is Google's social media platform and a direct competitor to Facebook, and works in a very similar way to Facebook. However, it has struggled to gain anything like the number of users that Facebook enjoys. Many news sites, blogs and other web presences have Google+ (G+) buttons that allow posts to be shared or liked in the same way as Facebook. Google+ allows users to connect, form communities of practice and research, communicate in video hangouts, post updates and create events, such as professional and personal community gatherings. Google+ data is captured by the likes of Altmetric.com.

LabRoots

LabRoots, launched in 2008, is a another academic network, focusing mainly on the scientific community. It allows users to create a personal profile and to follow topics of interest via various personal and news feeds. Visitors can access videos, job posts, references and other content without signing up for an account.

LinkedIn

Primarily a professional social network, LinkedIn has grown to have about 260 million users in around 200 countries and territories. It is particularly popular in the commercial professional sector, but many academics also have accounts. This has led to LinkedIn creating a higher education strand called Higher Ed Professionals. LinkedIn allows users to connect, have group discussions, post questions, advertise and discover jobs as well as to build an online professional profile. Content from around the web can be linked and shared through LinkedIn, giving it a higher profile. Many popular websites and blogs have a LinkedIn share button as standard. LinkedIn is potentially a useful tool for academics who want to forge connections in public and private organizations.

Mendeley

Mendeley is well established within the academic and altmetrics communities and has four main purposes. First and foremost, it is a reference management tool that works in ways very similar to EndNote, Zotero and ReadCube. Second, it is a social network for academics and other allied professionals – a cross between Facebook and iTunes for research. Third, it is a huge database of white papers, conference proceedings, book and journal references, and other kinds of grey literature that is searchable by other Mendeley users. Fourth, it is an altmetrics tool, in that it allows users to discover how many other users have a copy of a specific paper in their collection. Mendeley, like many other tools such as Evernote, comes in three different versions: a desktop version (the version most used); a web version that allows users to access their accounts while away from their computers; and a mobile version via iOS, Android and a third-party Kindle app called Kinsync.

How Mendeley can be used

Mendeley is a collection of many tools and it is worth taking advantage of this by ensuring that you use as many of them as possible. Its social network aspect is very good for researchers trying to find like-minded academics for potential collaboration. This search for connections with a global audience of researchers can be useful for uncovering other people's research and communicating your own outputs.

Piirus

Piirus is one of the newer, second wave of research social networks and has gained traction since starting in 2011 as Research Match. Run by the University of Warwick, it helps users to make connections both within their institution and further afield. Like other networking platforms, its main purpose is to improve your connections and potential collaborations and increase the visibility of your research.

ResearchGate

Alongside Academia.edu, ResearchGate is one of the larger and more established academic social networks, with about six million users. Like other research networks, it allows users to find and follow academics with the same interests. ResearchGate allows users to share their papers, ask questions, form groups and have private conversations, and has its own metrics system for each individual. There is also a job market and a tool to help researchers find the best journal in which to publish their paper, called Journal Finder. This allows users to copy and paste a paper abstract into the tool, which then suggests a suitable journal to publish in. Despite not always being accurate, it is certainly worth spending a few minutes to try it out.

Twitter

Twitter is probably the social media tool most used by academics across all disciplines. There are an incredible number of ways that it can be used in academic settings. The platform allows users to follow, share, discuss and communicate publicly and privately with their social networks and beyond. There are several important things to remember when using Twitter in a professional setting, as discussed in the previous chapter. Twitter is a very open tool, most conversations take place in public and they are limited to 140 characters. LIS professionals and researchers can use Twitter in a variety of ways, and here are just a few of them:

- Stay up to date with peers in your area of research.
- Follow events and conferences via their hashtags and join in the conversation.

- Communicate with colleagues and your personal network in short, succinct, informal messaging.
- Create personalized searches for topics you are interested in, using dashboard tools like TweetDeck or Hootsuite that will automatically feed new content to you.
- Use Lists to create lists of people and expertise so you can filter through your Twitter timeline.

Another useful aspect of Twitter in the academic and altmetrics setting is the great many tools that you can use to analyse your account. These allow you to see the reach of your tweets and profile, and those in your network, and helps you to make informed decisions about whom to follow and unfollow. A few of these tools are listed in the web resources at the end of this chapter. A couple of useful guides on how you can apply Twitter in an academic setting are also listed in the section on web resources.

Collaboration
Authorea
Authorea is a collaborative online writing tool for academics.

Google Docs
Google Docs is available to individuals or groups as part of a personal account or via the Google Apps for Education Suite for universities and colleges. It is Google's equivalent of word processing, spreadsheet and presentation software, and enables real-time collaboration across the web.

Hivebench
This allows scientists to create an online 'lab notebook' where they can conduct and analyse experiments in one place.

Overleaf

Overleaf allows researchers to collaborate using a rich-text editor as well as to write and edit directly in LaTeX. Manuscripts can be edited and reviewed directly in the cloud.

Audio and video
audioBoom

audioBoom (formerly known as audioBoo) is a micro-podcast site for your own recordings and can be considered as the audio equivalent of Twitter. The tool works across all platforms but is most useful on mobile devices. It allows you to make short audio recordings which you can then tag, add a picture to and geotag before uploading to your collection.

How audioBoom can be applied

A quick and simple way to apply audioBoom is to record short abstracts of your published research. You could just read the abstracts so that interested parties can listen to you talking about your work while they commute. An alternative, which may at first seem a little daunting, is to ask a colleague or someone from your marketing team to conduct a short interview about your work. audioBoom helps to break down your research into easily digestible artefacts that can be shared on social media.

Explain Everything

Explain Everything is a useful mobile app that allows users to screen-capture web content. It captures all of the actions carried out by the user, from navigating a website to zooming in and out. It is thus a quick and useful way to capture what a web page or website does. The video that is created can then be exported to a platform such as YouTube, Google Drive or Vimeo. It is a very simple tool and is much used in learning and teaching settings, but is also applicable in online instruction and training.

How Explain Everything can be applied

This app could be used by LIS professionals to create instructional videos to help academics understand and navigate various altmetrics tools such as figshare and Altmetric.com.

iTunes U

iTunes U, with the U standing for university, is Apple's academic equivalent of its popular iTunes marketplace of mobile apps, music, books, videos and podcasts. It allows academics and universities to host a variety of useful materials related to teaching and research. The content can be video recordings or audio podcasts and there are no restrictions on length. The materials can be stored in collections to which users subscribe and from which they can automatically receive notification of new additions. iTunes U is not blocked in countries where some of Apple's major competitors may be operating. It is not a platform for direct marketing of content such as courses, but is a place where academic content can be shared globally. Not every institution has an iTunes U account and accounts are not available to individuals, but if you work for a university that does subscribe to iTunes U it is worth encouraging academics to upload content to it. The iTunes U dashboard enables account managers to view downloads and play statistics for each collection and item.

How iTunes U can be applied

Video is becoming increasingly important in the academic community as a way to deliver ideas, research and knowledge, and podcasts are a very popular way for users to listen to content while on the go. Videos and podcasts do not need to be long. Examples of what could be uploaded in short videos include short tutorials, solutions to common problems and explanations of research strands such as information literacy.

Mixcloud

Mixcloud is primarily a DJ mix and podcasting site, although that should not put users off. It has diversified and has a section where seminars and lectures are hosted. Mixcloud is a very functional and good-looking site with social media sharing functionality. It also allows users to embed recordings into their own websites. Academic institutions such as the London School of Economics (LSE) and Stanford University host their content on Mixcloud. Like audioBoom, it lives outside the academic arena but nevertheless is a useful and easy-to-use option for uploading academic output.

Vimeo

Vimeo is a less popular but nonetheless good-quality alternative to YouTube. As with YouTube, users can upload video and audio recordings to the site and share them via links and social media. Vimeo has nothing like the amount of web traffic that YouTube enjoys, but it also has fewer adverts and, in my experience, less trolling and inappropriate material. Uploading to iTunes U gives your content academic credibility, and YouTube will bring you a potentially bigger audience. That said, if you have the time, also uploading your content to Vimeo is well advised. It takes very little time to upload content, and duplication with another site only becomes problematic when you choose to remove older content.

YouTube

YouTube is one of the web tools that most people will have heard of, alongside Google, Twitter and Facebook. It is the dominant video-hosting tool on the web and 300 hours of content are uploaded every minute of the day – a number that we can expect only to increase. It therefore makes sense, if you have any video and audio content, to upload it there. As for some of the other tools mentioned in this chapter, you can log into it from your Google account. If you work in an institution that has a GAFE (Google Apps for Education) Agreement, you can upload content either through your own account or via a shared one. You should check with your institution whether its GAFE Agreement covers YouTube and whether there is any risk of its being rescinded, and it is important always to know where the actual video files are stored, should you need to transfer them to another platform at a later date – which in reality is very unlikely.

Infographics and visualizations

It would be fair to say that research conference posters are not the most attractive of academic outputs. Usually they are shorter versions of the publication from which they were created. The rules on posters may have been relaxed somewhat at some conferences, but the majority still seem to be chunks of text with the introduction, methods and results copied and pasted onto a large sheet of paper or material. Added to this are the obligatory pixelated images taken from the web and the odd table or chart. Rarely do we see extended contact details, QR (quick response) codes, shortened, easy-to-copy URLs or social media links. There are also the non-conference posters, which do allow for more artistic licence, but even some of these can be as appealing to read as the terms and conditions for Facebook.

There are several tools that can be employed to deliver a striking and informative poster. At conference poster sessions often the hardest part is to lure delegates to walk over from the café area to view and discuss your work. A more colourful, inviting poster can help with that.

Infographics are, as the word suggests, both informative and graphic. They take key messages from a piece of information and turn them into an eye-catching, easy-to-digest poster. Some of the best examples can be viewed on David McCandless's website Information is Beautiful at www.informationisbeautiful.net/. Several tools offer a variety of infographic options, starting from basic, simple posters that can be exported, stored and printed; a fee may be charged for higher-resolution versions. Other non-infographic tools such as Google Slides and PowerPoint can also be used to make your posters more visually engaging.

Some infographics sites have now become marketplaces where designers can be commissioned to make an infographic. It is important to note that with any infographics tool you are likely to gain access only to the basic features and templates. While infographics are still gaining acceptance, there are already thousands of them on the web and this means that similar posters using the same templates are likely to appear.

The risk of turning up at a conference with a poster designed to the same template as someone else's can be reduced by paying for one of the premium templates or, if your funds will allow it, having someone design and create a poster from scratch.

The more prominent infographics tools are listed here for readers to explore. There are also several tools that researchers can use to host their posters and presentations. Most are very simple to use and they can be an effective way to host academic content and share via social networks.

F1000Posters

The F in F1000 stands for faculty, and F1000 has various strands, posters being one of them. It is an open repository of academic posters that can be linked to a journal paper and also allows for comments and feedback. Posters can be shared via various social networks and can be imported into a user's Mendeley account.

Figshare

Figshare is covered in gerneral terms in the section on altmetrics in this chapter. However, it is important to note that figshare hosts posters as part of its services. Academics are able to upload their posters (among other research artefacts) and then share them easily across their scholarly networks.

Impactstory

Impactstory, like figshare, is another multi-faceted altmetrics tool which also allows for the archiving of posters.

ScienceOpen Posters

ScienceOpen Posters is a repository of posters hosted on the research and publishing network.

SlideShare

SlideShare is one of the chief tools that academics should use to aid the discoverability of their research. SlideShare was acquired by LinkedIn in 2012 and allows users to upload documents, posters and presentations to the web. These materials can then be shared via social media and embedded into web pages and blogs. It is very simple to use and it takes only a few minutes to upload presentations, together with a brief description and tags to aid discoverability. The main point for researchers to consider is whether they have the rights to share a presentation and whether the materials breach any copyrights. The issue of copyright can at times be grey, but there are certain things that should not be used in presentations. Putting a copyright symbol on a slide that contains content taken from a place such as Getty Images does not make it legal. This is an instance of when the knowledgeable librarian can help. Advice can be given on the various copyright licences, in particular Creative Commons. There are also royalty-free image websites and those that require small fees to access their repository. Any academic library will have at least one librarian knowledgeable about copyright. All too often a presentation is filed away after being delivered. This is a missed opportunity when there may well be others on the web who would be interested to see it. Sharing presentations on SlideShare creates a post-talk 'legacy'. In addition, SlideShare provides analytics of things such as views and downloads.

Zenodo

Zenodo's primary purpose is to share a variety of research results from across all fields of science. As well as being a digital repository for text, spreadsheets, audio and video, it also hosts research posters.

While some of the tools reviewed here may not be purely for academic use, that does not mean that they should be excluded. One of the aims of this book is to improve the process of scholarly communication, and if that involves encouraging academics to share content in the places where potential users are to be found, then it makes sense to go there, even though measurement and academic feedback are less likely to happen. There is no reason not to share research posters via popular image-hosting websites such as Flickr and Pinterest, if the content and subject matter are accessible enough.

Blogging and informal modes of communication

Blogging has been part of the academic communication cycle for some time. It is far from new within the research and LIS sectors, and has come a long way from the early, text-heavy versions that appeared in the late 1990s. For a while it seemed that blogging was in decline as social media and video started to gain in popularity. But blogging is still very much alive, and an excellent platform for sharing and discussing ideas and research with peers and a wider audience. This may partly result from the growth of the WordPress support community, who use the WordPress package not just to run blogs but also to build websites. While Blogger remains a very popular tool, blogging was given a shot in the arm when Tumblr appeared as an alternative to the blogging heavyweights.

Blogging is a superb way to convert your formal research into an easier-to-digest, informal summary. It also provides good practice in writing summaries of your work for the lay reader, condensing original content of, say, 6000 words into just 600 words. Some academics regard this as 'dumbing down' their serious work. However, while impact is undeniably an inherent part of the research process, blogging aids the job of getting research out to existing and new professional and public audiences.

LSE Impact Blog

Anyone who is interested in the area of scholarly communication and impact should look at the LSE's blogging platforms, in particular its Impact Blog. It is a valuable resource for sharing advice and ideas closely related to altmetrics and other ways of measuring and communicating research. The blog accepts guest articles, so if you are a blogger and are interested in the topics in this book, it is worth pitching an article idea to it.

The Conversation

The Conversation is an online publication that pairs up academics with journalists to write news articles based on their areas of expertise. The Conversation started in Australia, then launched in the UK and now has US and African editions. It is a great way for academics to share content with a wider audience beyond the bounds of the university. The format is simple: the academic submits a short pitch based on what they would like to write about. If an editor in that topic area likes it, they request a longer article, usually under 1000 words. The article is then edited by journalists to a style that is more in line with a piece that you would read in a newspaper such as the *Guardian* or *The Times*. The revised article is then returned to the academic for approval. Once agreed, the article is published and the academic has access to an internal dashboard that includes tweets, comments and views posted by readers.

Altmetrics and other metrics
Altmetric.com

As its name suggests, Altmetric is in the business of scholarly measurement and communication. Chapter 5 in this book is written by Altmetric.com founder and CEO Euan Adie and covers much of what Altmetric.com's remit is. As with other tools focused mostly on altmetrics, its aim is to offer not something that is wholly different from traditional metrics, but supplementary information. These alternative indicators include tweets, blog posts and news media coverage, among others. One of the criticisms of traditional metrics, in particular of citations, is that they take a very long time to accrue. By a year or two after publication a quality research paper may still have accrued only a couple of citations shortly after publication – and that if it is lucky. The existing citation system provides very little feedback to authors as to how their research has been received and how far it may have spread globally.

The focus of Altmetric.com is on articles, not journals. Altmetric.com and its bookmarklet tool provide up-to-date information from a wide range of social media and web sources. On social media these include: Twitter, Facebook, Google+, Pinterest, Sina Weibo and blogs; and in traditional media they include both mainstream (e.g. *Guardian, New York Times*) and science-specific (*New Scientist, Scientific American*) journalism.

In addition, Altmetric.com sources cover many non-English titles. It monitors reference management tools such as CiteULike and Mendeley and other sources such as Wikipedia, YouTube, PubPeer, reddit, Publons and Reviews on F1000. Altmetric.com takes this data and creates a doughnut-shaped visual with various coloured bands that indicate where the posts mentioning the article have come from. For example, red indicates that the article has been mentioned in the mainstream media, blue that it has been tweeted about. You can drill down into the data to see where the media coverage has happened and who has tweeted about the article. You can also see geographical information, as it is important not only to know who is talking and writing about your research but also where they are located. All of the data is collated and used to create an altmetric score that appears in the centre of the doughnut. The score is weighted and ranges from 8 points for news coverage to 0.25 points for mentions in LinkedIn, reddit, Pinterest, YouTube and Facebook.[1]

Altmetric.com also provides what it calls their Explorer bookmarklet, which gives an altmetric breakdown and score for any papers in PubMed, arXiv or pages that contain a DOI. Researchers make up just part of the potential Altmetric.com user base; the data is also used by fund holders and publishers to monitor the influence and impact of the research they fund and publish.

Figshare

Like Altmetric.com, figshare is a platform at the forefront of the open research movement. Started by Mark Hahnel in 2011, it is an online repository of digital research artefacts. These can be figures, datasets, posters, presentations, images and videos, and they are free to use. In 2012 Digital Science stepped into support the fledgling platform, which has continued to gain traction in the research and library communities. Figshare is now in partnership with PLOS and offers an institutional repository service. Another partnership was established in 2013, with fellow altmetrics-led company Impactstory. The success of figshare is widely acknowledged by the research community and the fact that it made 200,000 files publicly available in its first year is a clear statement of its intent. By September 2013 the number had risen to over one million artefacts. Figshare allows users to upload files in any format for dissemination across the web. Uploaded data can be made private or public and the current limit on individual private space is set at 1 gigabyte. Figshare also promotes the uploading of negative data, making everything that researchers do citable with a DOI. Academia has not always taken best advantage of cloud-based packages, but figshare allows users to access their content anywhere on the web. At the time of writing it is offering a variety of packages that would satisfy even the most data hungry of researchers.

Harzing Publish or Perish

This is not an altmetric tool as such, but a software program that can retrieve and analyse academic citations. It uses Google Scholar and Microsoft Academic Search to seek out raw citations and then analyses them to provide a collection of metrics. Some of these metrics include the contemporary h index, Egghie's g index, Hirsch's h index, average citations per paper, citations per author, papers per author and citations per year.

Impactstory

The tagline on Impactstory's home page is 'Your CV, but better'. Like figshare, it started life in 2011 and is one of the champions of the open research and altmetrics movement. The platform was set up by Jason Priem and Heather Piwowar on the back of a hackathon project at the Beyond Impact Workshop in 2011. It was afterwards, during a 24-hour coding marathon, that the collaboration and platform was born. Impactstory takes a philanthropic approach to its funding and is not for profit. It is driven by open source and the idea of free and open data, to the extent permitted by data providers. As with other key altmetrics providers, there is a high level of transparency and open communication. Unlike many of today's formal academic hosting platforms, journals or otherwise, Impactstory gives users full control over their data, and anyone who wishes to stop using the site can export their data at any time. The Impactstory software that hosts it is fully open source. Individuals who create a profile on Impactstory can see the impact of their content spread across articles, datasets, figures, posters, slide decks and software products. Visitors to an academic's profile can drill down into their data and see download statistics, geographical information, tweets and views on Impactstory and figshare. Impactstory also shows at what percentile the artefact is ranked on Impactstory. Additional data shows citation, viewing and discussion activity for articles, so that a researcher can gain a quick view of how their work is being received on the web. Software products are also measured using GitHub and Impactstory; in addition to citations and views these products can also have a varying level of recommendations.

Klout

The aim of most of the academic tools and resources reviewed in this book is to improve the impact of research communication and measurement. Klout, which is not an exclusively academic tool, can be used to measure social media reach and influence on a variety of platforms. Like Altmetric.com, Klout creates a score based on a person's impact on social media from a starting point, not their research output per se. The more you use Klout, and the more expert you become, the higher your score will go. To some extent you have power to influence your score, more so than with Altmetric.com. For example, if you tweet about your work and it gets retweeted by others that aids your score, but you still need to tweet it. The Klout Score runs from 1 to 100, and the more influential you are, the higher your Klout Score. Klout looks at a variety of networks, including Facebook, Twitter, LinkedIn and Instagram. It does not look at academically focused platforms such as ResearchGate and SlideShare.

Kred

Like Kudos (see below), Kred focuses on mainstream social media and uses the data to create a score to measure a person's influence.

Kudos

Kudos explains its remit as being to help researchers to explain, enrich and share their publications for greater research impact. As with some of the other platforms covered in this chapter, its goal is to help researchers get discovered, read and cited. It is now allied with Altmetric.com to include Altmetric.com's metrics as part of its package. Kudos works with several publishers, including major ones such as Taylor & Francis and Wiley. As with Altmetric.com, Kudos also seeks to provide metrics for publishers and fundholders so that they can gain a better picture of the influence and impact of the research that they fund and publish.

Lazy Scholar

Lazy Scholar was created by PhD student Colby Vorland and works as a Firefox, Opera or Chrome extension. It allows users to collate a number of metrics, including altmetric, journal impact and Web of Science scores, as well as links to full text and author contact details. The extension does not always pull in the full data – which is generally because it is not available in the first place. However, it is a useful and quick-to-use tool for checking the metrics – new and old – of a paper.

Mendeley

Mendeley is covered in Chapter 6 and so there is little need for detailed coverage here. Mendeley is many things: a repository of research, a social network, a reference management tool; and it has its own alternative metric of how many Mendeley users have saved a specific reference. Mendeley can be regarded as the Google Docs of reference management tools, in that it has taken an existing and useful tool such as reference management and given it a Web 2.0 makeover. The result is a cloud-based, social, constantly evolving technology. The development of Web 2.0 and social technologies, and academics' growing desire to access research while on the go using mobile and web-based platforms gave rise to reference management tools like CiteULike, Connotea and Zotero. Shortly after their creation another technology appeared by the name of Mendeley, which was the first to properly bridge the gap between web and desktop reference management.

Mendeley works like any traditional and modern reference management package, and users can add a variety of references to their database in a variety of ways. They can add references manually, import them from journal databases and use Mendeley's own web importer tool, which extracts selected results from sources such as Google Scholar and PubMed. Users can also instruct their Mendeley account to look at a watched folder for any new PDFs that they place in it, and can also drag and drop PDFs into their account. The reason for mentioning Mendeley here is that it has a real interest in the data that is generated by its users. One important strand of that data is who is saving papers to their accounts, which becomes an altmetric. If a paper is saved by hundreds of Mendeley users this may mean that it is a very good paper, one that may be cited. Certainly, if a paper is in a reference management database such as Mendeley it has more chance of being cited than if it was just tucked away on a shelf. Mendeley is able to drill down into a host of different statistics that show who has saved a paper by discipline, geographical location and career demographics.

PLOS Article Level Metrics

The Public Library of Science (PLOS) looks at a wide range of Article Level Metrics (ALMs) for articles that have been published in its own journals. These can be usage statistics such as PLOS and PubMed Central views and downloads in PDF and XML format. Citations are counted from PubMed Central, CrossRef, Scopus and Web of Science. Other platforms and social networks are also monitored, including CiteULike, Mendeley, Twitter and Facebook. In addition, PLOS looks at the comments that are left on publications, and notes and ratings in its own database of research. Finally, PLOS ALMs takes into consideration blogs and media including Nature Blogs, ScienceSeeker, Wikipedia and trackbacks from elsewhere on the web. The aim of these metrics is to aid researchers and their institutions, as well as funders and publishers, to understand the scholarly reach and impact of their work.

Plum Analytics

Plum Analytics, now part of EBSCO Information Services, aims to track and assess the impact of research. Plum Analytics categorizes its metrics into five separate types: usage, captures, mentions, social media and citations. The platform looks at a long list of metrics that covers usage statistics including downloads, full text and abstract views, in addition to clicks, among other things. These are retrieved from tools such as figshare, GitHub, EBSCO and Dryad. Other things measured include bookmarks on Delicious, and favourites on SlideShare and YouTube. Data about who has a particular artefact in their collection is captured via websites such as Mendeley and Goodreads. Mentions and comments from Facebook, reddit, SlideShare, Vimeo and YouTube are also included. The list is very extensive and can be explored further on Plum Analytics' metrics web page.

Snowball Metrics

Snowball Metrics' agenda is to create a set of metrics that are defined and agreed by research-intensive universities. Its long-term aim is to create a global set of standards that are not tied to any particular provider of data or tools. Like the other metrics-focused platforms mentioned above, Snowball Metrics does not aim to replace peer review or expert opinion. It is another set of alternative indicators that works alongside existing models of scholarly measurement.

Other notable academic tools

The number of web technologies and tools that researchers can use to measure and communicate their research is growing rapidly. Added to that are the many other useful tools for managing, citing, hosting and collaborating on research. In fact there are simply too many to mention here, and by the time you read this chapter it is likely that dozens more will have appeared on the web. The following is a list of just a few of the more useful tools that LIS professionals should consider encouraging academics to use:

- CiteULike
- DataCite
- Dryad

- Google Scholar
- ORCiD
- ReadCube
- Research Compendia
- ShareLaTeX
- WriteLaTeX.

Conclusion

All the tools reviewed in this chapter can aid scholarly communication in some way, although not all of them can be labelled as altmetrics, which can be open to different interpretations. Impact, copyright, big data and open access may be seen by different people as different things. Only a few of the tools reviewed here are truly altmetric. Many of them, such as Twitter, are instrumental in providing the data for some of the purely altmetric tools, and are themselves providing altmetric scores. If a researcher tweets a paper and that paper is retweeted by others, that provides some kind of figure, although someone's tweeting about your latest research does not mean that they will read it. The same can be said of someone's downloading your paper from an institutional repository – there is no guarantee that it will be read or even cited. It could mean, however, that there is a greater chance that these things will happen. By sharing your research on some of these platforms or across the variety of channels there is more chance that it will be viewed, shared, downloaded and possibly cited. The biggest problem for any LIS professional or academic is in choosing the ones in which to invest time. It is hoped that this chapter has helped to clear the water rather than to muddy it.

Key points

As in so many areas of research, there are a growing number of technologies that can be used by LIS professionals and academics. The growth in breadth and depth of these technologies does not show any sign of slowing down. Altmetrics is just part of the equation and many of the tools covered in this chapter help to shape it. There are many choices for LIS professionals and academics when deciding where to invest their time and energy in using new technologies.

Note

1   Information on the Altmetric.com score can be viewed at:
    http://support.altmetric.com/knowledgebase/articles/83337-how-is-the-
    altmetric-score-calculated.

Web resources
Social networks

https://about.me/
https://www.academia.edu/
www.biomedexperts.com/
https://en-gb.facebook.com/
https://plus.google.com/
https://itunes.apple.com/gb/app/mendeley-pdf-reader/id380669300?mt=8
www.kinsync.com/
http://labroots.com/
https://uk.linkedin.com/
https://university.linkedin.com/
https://www.mendeley.com/
https://play.google.com/store/apps/details?id=com.mendeley
https://www.piirus.com/
https://www.researchgate.net
https://www.researchgate.net/publicliterature.PublicLiteratureSearch.html
https://twitter.com.

Useful tools for managing Twitter

Social Media Analytics: https://sumall.com/.
Manage your Twitter followers: https://manageflitter.com/.
Turn other's tweets into a daily news briefing: www.news.me/.
Turn your and others' tweets into a daily news page:
    http://paper.li/?utm_expid=72755654–17.m4jg63hLTw2rNg4T1M9buw.0.
Create a Twitter dashboard of timelines, keyword searches and mentions:
    https://hootsuite.com/.
Another useful aggregate tool like Hootsuite, from Twitter:
    https://tweetdeck.twitter.com/.

Guides on how to use Twitter

LSE Guide: Using Twitter in university research, teaching, and impact activities:
   http://blogs.lse.ac.uk/impactofsocialsciences/2011/09/29/twitter-guide/.
Twitter Guide Book – How to, tips and instructions by Mashable:
   http://mashable.com/guidebook/twitter/.

Collaboration

https://www.authorea.com/
https://docs.google.com
https://www.hivebench.com/
https://www.overleaf.com/.

Audio and video

https://audioboom.com/
http://explaineverything.com/
www.apple.com/uk/education/ipad/itunes-u/
https://www.mixcloud.com/
https://vimeo.com/.

Infographics

Easel.ly: www.easel.ly/.
Gapminder: www.gapminder.org/.
Infogr.am: https://infogr.am/.
Many Eyes: www-01.ibm.com/software/analytics/many-eyes/.
Piktochart: https://magic.piktochart.com/.
Plot.ly: https://plot.ly/feed/.
Visual.ly: http://visual.ly/.

Presentations and posters

http://f1000research.com/
http://figshare.com/article_types
https://impactstory.org/

https://www.scienceopen.com/collection/scienceopen_posters
www.slideshare.net/
https://zenodo.org/collection/posters.

Blogging and informal modes of communication

http://blogs.lse.ac.uk/impactofsocialsciences/
https://theconversation.com/uk.

Altmetrics

www.altmetric.com/
http://figshare.com/
www.harzing.com/pop.htm
https://impactstory.org/about
https://klout.com/home
http://home.kred/
https://www.growkudos.com/about/
www.lazyscholar.org/
https://www.mendeley.com/
http://article-level-metrics.plos.org/
http://plumanalytics.com/
www.snowballmetrics.com/.

Other useful web resources

Useful websites for staying up to date with scholarly communications and platforms:

101 Innovations in Scholarly Communication – the Changing Research Workflow: http://figshare.com/articles/101_Innovations_in_Scholarly_Communication_the_Changing_Research_Workflow/1286826.

400+ Tools and Innovations in Scholarly Communication: https://docs.google.com/spreadsheets/d/1KUMSeq_Pzp4KveZ7pb5rddcssk1XBTiLHniD0d3nDqo/edit#gid=1519702055.

Altmetric Blog: www.altmetric.com/blog/.

Eventbrite: https://www.eventbrite.co.uk/.

Digital Science Blog: www.digital-science.com/blog/.

figshare Blog: http://figshare.com/blog.

Impactstory Blog: http://blog.impactstory.org/.

iTunes U: https://itunes.apple.com/gb/itunes-u/scharr-research-hacks/
    id985562918?mt=10.

Kudos Blog: http://blog.mendeley.com/.

LSE Impact Blog: http://blogs.lse.ac.uk/impactofsocialsciences/.

Mendeley Blog: http://blog.mendeley.com/.

ScHARR Research Hacks: https://www.youtube.com/playlist?list=
    PL1mJ7IZ3qFxjR8HhL9HX-ETHUFJz639Bt.

Further reading

Carter, R., Wood, A. and Bancroft, D. (2013) *The Legal Side of Blogging: how not to get sued, fired, arrested, or killed*, 3rd edn, JENTS.

McCandless, D. (2009) *Information is Beautiful*, Harper Collins.

Raubenheimer, J. (2014) *Mendeley: crowd-sourced reference and citation management in the information era*, True Insight Publishing.

CHAPTER 9

The connected academic: implementing altmetrics within your organization

Andy Tattersall

Introduction

LIS professionals can experience major problems in implementing change, especially in academia. Reduced budgets are one reason for this, but the cultural fabric of their organizations and fields of practice are the principal problem. When you are trying to change organizational practice it is common to come up against a myriad of reasons why colleagues and students are reluctant to explore new ways of working. This chapter will look at the two issues facing LIS professionals in the task of providing their organizations with relevant skills and knowledge in relation to altmetrics.

Part 1 Getting the horse to water

First is the cultural and organizational resistance, usually identified at an individual level, that is built around time constraints, apathy, lack of technology awareness and absence of support. The first part of the chapter will look at different ways in which LIS professionals can engage with and encourage users to adopt a new technology or way of thinking with regard to altmetrics.

Part 2 Staying on track

The second part of the chapter will look at methods of support for instructors and academics when applying altmetrics to their work. Given that academics and students are increasingly busy with deadlines, commitments such as meetings and the growing pressure of e-mail and other information overload, it is essential not to further burden their workloads with non-essential distractions. This part will look at the issue of information and technology overload and the effects on attention span, workflow and output, and will provide a collection of solutions and methods to help those using altmetrics to do so in an effortless and streamlined way.

PART 1 GETTING THE HORSE TO WATER

LIS professionals will come across a wide range of groups and individuals as part of their role to help and support users. Those working on the front line will respond to a multitude of enquiries and requests and these interactions offer LIS professionals an ideal opportunity to build both their own and their customers' skill sets as they are often asked to investigate a new or unsolved problem, often using technology such as social media.

Altmetrics offers many opportunities for LIS professionals to showcase their skills. Librarians have been active on the web since its inception, and increasingly, since the development of Web 2.0, on social media. Many LIS staff use these technologies in a way that extends beyond the workplace to out-of-hours professional and social networks. They blog, tweet and have actual weekend meet-ups to talk about library technologies and policies. A good example is the unconference event Library Camp, where those with an interest in libraries meet at weekends. My point here is that many advocates at such initiatives are willing to put in the extra time to discuss their field of work and interests. The same can be said about technologies and librarians: librarians spend much of their own time investigating new tools that they can use in their own work. They are also interested in information literacy, copyright, critical appraisal and good practice, all of which they can translate to researchers through their own role within the library.

If you are an academic LIS professional it is likely that you will come into direct contact with academics, teachers and students. And if you have a natural interest in technology, it is also likely that some of the people you work with will share your interest in developing technologies and the use of social media. That said, the majority of researchers are either happy working as they already are, or are blissfully unaware that, thanks to social media and technologies, their world is changing. Roger's Theory of the Diffusion of Innovation states that the majority of users of technologies and innovations embrace a new technology after the minority of innovators and early adopters have done so. The take-up of a new technology relies heavily on four elements: the actual innovation (in this case, altmetrics); the communication channels, which for a large part operate within social media and therefore can be a barrier for those not using them; time, which we will discuss further on; and a social system, which is the organization or the wider group with which the LIS professional is trying to engage.

The problem for academia, and to some extent for altmetrics, is that a huge shift is happening that has the potential to affect every researcher, teacher and student in the future. The main protagonists are MOOCs and open access, and there has also been a rapid growth of interest in information and digital literacy. Add to this the continued expansion of social media and mobile learning as a means of communication, alongside that of altmetrics, and professional support staff have a lot to consider. Those working in more focused roles will find it easier to decide how to use their time and efforts to support their peers and academics; others may be overwhelmed by the changes going on around them and the demands to help others to adapt to them. There are also increasing demands on researchers to create better-quality research and more of it and, more recently, to measure the impact of their research. The majority of academics may not be aware of the implications of these shifts, and working practices may continue as they are for many years before we see a widespread technology-driven change.

Before undertaking any kind of development, support and outreach work in relation to something that can appear wholly alien to a large percentage of academics and allied professionals, it is only realistic to expect the degree of success in some areas to be limited. This is especially so in the case of anyone working on their own or across different teams and departments. Those working in liaison, technical specialist, subject specific, development and impact roles often work in isolation for long periods of time. This means they are a finite resource, and a big shift in working practices using technology can take up a lot of that time, not only to deploy the technology but also to understand it. Therefore it is important to understand your limitations and where you can achieve quick wins, and to highlight what can use up your time unproductively. The following quote from Benjamin Franklin typifies what many agents of change encounter in their daily roles: 'All mankind is divided into three classes: those that are immovable, those that are movable, and those that move.'

Those with limited resources and time should aim to work with the latter two groups identified by Franklin (2007). By identifying those that 'move' you will be able to make connections with useful champions who in turn will help to promote altmetrics to those who are movable. Anyone who facilitates any kind of change within an organization through staff development and the take-up of something like altmetrics needs to know how far their resources and patience can stretch. Trying to bring about a change in how people work and use technology can be exhausting, and too many defeats can have a negative effect on the morale of the teacher. By better understanding the academics with whom you work, you can reduce the number of defeats by avoiding the battles you are never likely to win.

Altmetrics and social media – a blurring of boundaries

One of the biggest challenges facing LIS professionals in persuading academics and students to engage with altmetrics is the fact that some of the tools cross over professional and personal boundaries. Consider some of the tools that are used to create the metrics within altmetrics – Facebook and Twitter being good examples. If you consider two of their most important components – Likes and tweets and how they are applied – and then transfer these to an academic setting you can understand why researchers have some reservations. This is because Facebook and Twitter are for the most part considered personal social media tools and, more importantly, personal spaces. Consider who is most renowned for using Twitter, such as Stephen Fry with his six million followers; or how Facebook is used for mass advertising of products based on algorithms derived from personal data from discussions, Likes and Shares. This creates a huge barrier for academics, the majority of whom have spent their careers working in the protective domain of academia. Universities are referred to as ivory towers, in that they remove academics from everyday life. Social media is the opposite, in that it puts people in the spotlight of everyday life.

Social media within altmetrics works on connectivity, communities and measurement of the information and data that are hosted and shared via the various platforms. It is a system of sharing and highlighting research – not always good research – and aids a quicker and simpler communication process. Social media reflects much of what happens in real life, in that it captures the good, the bad and the ugly. At any given moment on Facebook people are sharing kind words, funny web links and hateful messages. This can be a cause of concern for anyone who decides to take the step from using social media on a personal level to employing it on a professional one, or from a position of not using it at all.

Academics need evidence

Academic research can be quite a laborious and methodical process, and one that must be underpinned as much as possible by evidence. This way of working is instilled into academics from their time as university students. They will have been taught to question hypotheses, and not take things at face value. With regard to embracing altmetrics and technologies as a whole, they may have a variety of questions that the LIS professional will have to answer:

- What are the benefits?
- Is this a good use of my time?
- Is this system good quality?
- Is this system stable?
- What are the pitfalls?
- Why use this technology, could it just be a fad?

What are the benefits?

This topic is covered in other chapters of this book and is covered here in tandem with the second question: is it a good use of my time? A couple of real-life scenarios will be used to illustrate both ends of the spectrum that academic librarians may encounter.

Is this a good use of my time?

A problem many of us have is using our time more productively and efficiently, especially given the growing demands of modern lifestyles on our time and attention. The answer to the question may lie in who is asking why they should work in different way. We have to remember that even though many academics use social media on a personal level, they can struggle to make the transition to its professional use. There are some tools that academics will see as very personal (Facebook, Instagram and FourSquare), and others that are professional – such as Mendeley, ResearchGate and LinkedIn. The problem is that some of the tools sit between the personal and professional. These include Twitter, YouTube and Google+, among others. The first two highlight what a confusing world social media is with regard to altmetrics. Twitter is extensively used by celebrities and the media, and there are high-profile stories featuring celebrities, sports people and politicians who have publicly fallen foul of its misuse. It is likely that academics have come across these stories, which will contribute to their reservations and fears and pose a barrier to the use of social media in an academic setting. But what we have to remember is that, for the most part, no one expects academics to engage with social media and altmetrics, and that in choosing to engage they may be taking a leap of faith.

The following two scenarios will help to decide whether using altmetrics and social media is a good use of time.

Scenario 1

An academic asks 'Is this a good use of my time?' They are a couple of decades into their career, a senior academic, possibly a professor, and have published several papers in high-impact, peer-reviewed journals. They are thinking about engaging with social media and altmetrics but are not sure whether it would actually benefit their career at this stage. Senior, established academics are more likely to be interested in what is happening in their field and in the discussions taking place on social media than in improving the citations of their papers, as they will have already gained plenty of recognition in this area.

Senior academics engaging with altmetrics and social media carry more influence than their junior colleagues and they may have come across peers who are using social media and altmetrics as part of their own learning and impact agenda. It is highly likely that some of their peers will be active on Twitter, so this is a good place to start and something about which the LIS professional can find evidence for them. A good starting place is to find out who from your own institution– but also, more importantly, at other institutions – is actively tweeting about their work. It is particularly useful to find those who are actively debating and open for conversation about research topics that your senior academic is interested in. Given that there is also a competitive element to academia and publishing, tools like Twitter will gain credibility with some if they are viewed as a massive, multi-level computer game in which users try to achieve new goals via followers and retweets. That said, the real benefits come from finding useful research, sharing content, promoting your own outputs, forming networks and having discussions.

If you are able to help your senior academic to build their network of peers and useful resources, the next challenge will be to help them manage their time and identify what they can actually start to share online. We will cover that below. One good way to go about getting users to engage with Twitter is to explain it like this: 'There is a conversation about a topic that interests you, whether you decide to join the conversation is up to you.'

So, while using social media to improve citations may not be of the greatest importance to more established academics, it could be a fruitful route into discovering new hot topics and debating them with established peers and new global audiences.

Scenario 2

An early career researcher who uses social media every day, mostly for personal interactions, wants to use social media and altmetrics in their professional life. They have some idea about the basics but are also concerned that their line manager, who is an older, established academic, might perceive the use of such tools as not constituting work.

The evidence shows that those who have set up altmetrics-focused companies – figshare, Mendeley, Altmetric.com, Impactstory, etc. – and others pushing the altmetrics agenda are usually younger, PhD-level, early career researchers. So, your early career researcher is not alone and may have the same reasons for investigating altmetrics as those who originally started the platforms. For example, they may have datasets that they want to share publicly for others to use, they may wish to share their research via a blog or to open up discussion with their peers on Twitter. To some extent the force of technology change is driving this agenda, as is a desire on the part of early career researchers to modify or change an established system of research dissemination and evaluation. There is evidence of this in other changes in academia, such as open access and MOOCs, where some of those leading the charge are doing so either for altruistic reasons or because they want to shake up a somewhat ossified academia. To some extent, there is an underlying ethos that there is 'nothing to lose' among those who have not yet established their research careers. But for a young academic on their first contract in a research facility it can feel risky to work in a way that seems alien to their departmental colleagues.

Once again, the answer is to provide evidence as to the benefits for the user, as well as time management tools for altmetrics. As in the first example, the researcher can benefit by creating social connections, except in this instance they may focus on following the influencers in their research field as well as their peers. The influencers may be journal editors, established academics, professionals and organizations. By getting involved in the conversation that is happening in their area of research they can begin to establish potential networks and future collaboration. With a little ground work the young academic can start to broadcast their own work and expertise to the web and start to have conversations that they might otherwise never have, even at an international conference. Social media is a great icebreaker; it allows users to make brief, informal opening contact with others. An ideal use is at conferences, especially if the junior academic is following the conference hashtag. By replying to tweets from other delegates they have the possibility to open up channels of communication that can last well after the conference has ended.

The time issue is key, especially when careers can be defined by the worryingly short sentence of 'publish or perish'. There is real pressure on early career researchers to maintain a consistently good-quality standard of work in order to move up within their field of research, and, obviously, to work very hard. Altmetrics, if used wisely, has the potential to afford those developments to establish contacts and discover useful knowledge. The problem is that managing these extra communication streams can be seen as a distraction from the work that the researcher has been contracted to do. A useful solution here is to manage the times when a user communicates or shares something interesting. There are tools that allow users to schedule their tweets, such as TweetDeck, their blog posts, such as Blogger, and even their e-mails, Boomerang for Gmail being one example. Another useful strategy is to use mobile devices more fluently. Many academics now have smartphones, and an increasing number have tablet devices. These mobile devices allow users to interact, stay abreast of research and share ideas while travelling or in between commitments, and remove the need to be behind a desk in order to do all of this. The modern work force is increasingly mobile, working while travelling, at home and at conferences and in hotels. Some of this time can be used in building and establishing academic networks and sharing ideas and published work. By using some of the shortcuts available thanks to technology with tools such as F1000, TweetDeck and Google Docs, researchers will be better placed to engage with altmetrics without disrupting their active research time.

Is this system good quality?

This is perhaps the hardest question of all to answer. A large factor in the appearance of altmetrics was that many felt the existing methods, citations, impact factors, etc. not only failed to capture everything but also did not always highlight quality research. Yet the question is being asked, does altmetrics work and does it highlight quality? It is understandable that when a new system appears users will wish to scrutinize it and test it out. This is especially the case in academia, where there is a strong need for a good evidence base and debate and criticism come with the territory. Any kind of new technology and innovation goes through the Hype Cycle curve, where the new idea is first lauded, and then dissected and pulled apart by critics. In the case of altmetrics, the various platforms have gone through a period where interest has been positive, for the most part; but with that comes more criticism as some look to uncover the technology's shortcomings. If interest in altmetrics and backing from publishers and researchers and their institutions continues to grow, we may see the curve start to flatten out into what Gartner would refer to as the plateau of productivity – but that may still be some years away.

The question of whether altmetrics provides quality, or an improvement on the existing systems, is only starting to be answered. Research has been undertaken by various academics and the conclusions are varied. Some see altmetrics as the one-stop shop for measuring academic output, others see it as becoming something else in time, while detractors see it as nothing more than a fad. Detractors of altmetrics see it merely as a distraction or as an attention-measurement tool: a distraction to researchers and their work, or a tool for measuring the attention of readers and viewers, not the actual quality of the research. Some critics are concerned that altmetrics measures and rewards a researcher's ability to communicate, not the quality of their research. Certainly, the way research is measured will continue to change as we continue to change how we produce, share and find research outputs. We are talking about research on the web more than we have ever done; from academic blogs such as The Conversation to Twitter hashtags, discussion fills every second of every day.

The tools and systems that have been created to carry out and measure impact and sharing are of good quality and work very well. Mendeley was bought for an estimated $100m by Elsevier in 2013 and is widely respected as an excellent academic network, research discovery and management tool. Altmetric.com established collaborations with Springer and ScienceOpen in 2014, while Impactstory receives funding from the National Science Foundation in the USA. A more relevant question than that of quality is perhaps whether are there too many tools and systems, while the biggest problem for academics, fundholders and administrators may be that an already overburdened formal research system may become increasingly so as more technologies appear.

That said, systems evolve. The current ways of measuring research have been with us for some time and various tools, such as figshare and Mendeley, have shown that they do not measure well the breadth and depth of current research outputs. What organizations such as the Higher Education Funding Council for England (HEFCE) will do with the outputs from new tools and systems, and how this will affect the research community and society as a whole is a question that has not yet been fully answered.

Is the system stable?

It is important to know not just whether systems will remain stable and online, but also whether they will be around in years to come. Universities and research facilities have become increasingly reliant on third-party software hosted outside the establishment, and this has grown with the advent of cloud computing. Many academics are now using social media as part of their work – tools like ResearchGate, Twitter and CiteULike to name but a few. These tools host information about the user, their professional interests, thoughts and ideas, and are very unlike the previous ways of working where all of this content was often stored on a single, local hard drive. The concerns for researchers moving more towards the cloud and the use of social media and altmetrics are usually the following:

1 Is my data secure?
2 Who is behind this platform?
3 Who owns my content?
4 Will it still be here in the future?

These are usually the biggest concerns that any researcher will have when using third-party applications, and in many cases they have no concerns. If we consider the widespread use of Facebook, with over one billion users, we can safely say that, despite many having concerns about privacy and the changes that Facebook makes to it, the majority of users have never read its terms and conditions of use. The same can be said for most tools used in a professional setting. There is no big concern about the majority of these tools; the real problems with online technologies arise when they involve your bank details or personal home information.

Many web-based software providers have service level agreements (SLAs) which state the level of service you can expect from them. This can include the expected amount of down-time over the course of the year, or the estimated length of time they will take to resolve problems users may have. It is very unlikely that any software provider would offer to be online 100% of the time in the SLA. Since the advent of cloud computing, web hosting and data storage has become much more reliable and it is rare for third-party tools, especially established ones like ResearchGate and Mendeley, to go offline for more than very short periods.

As to whether your data is secure, this depends on what kind of data you are putting out. Is it personal data that you would not be willing to share? Is it research data that is sensitive, such as patient data? Often websites and companies are targeted for information relating to users' personal details – for example, their home address and bank details. Most altmetric tools do not capture this information, as the majority are free, while others such as Mendeley have secure payment methods for their premium versions. With any online account you set up it is important to assess the security measures that the platform has in place. The rule of thumb is to apply common sense. If you want to use a platform like figshare to host your data, it is important to ensure that it is data that you can host on a third-party tool.

The first three questions listed above can be answered by reading the terms and conditions and 'about us' pages of altmetric tools. Many of these tools are now allied with academic institutions, publishers and fund holders, and this at least gives some reassurance as to their motives and stability.

As more and more tools and applications appear on the web for academics and LIS professionals to use, the more people will ask which one to invest time in. Chapter 8 will help to answer that question, and it is hoped that the tools will be around in the future – although nothing can be guaranteed and some Web 2.0 tools have disappeared without trace; useful tools like Pageflakes and ScreenToaster, both used in academic and library settings, being good examples. However, many of the applications that academics use, such as Mendeley and Twitter, have millions of users and have created sustainable business models. Many are funded by publishers or by premium paid accounts, and many of the tools covered in this book have been around for almost a decade, with no signs of going out of business. Technologies in academia are a growing business and although some of the tools are not directly involved in altmetrics, the increased interaction by many of them with their API development and collaborations helps sustain their future as they become intertwined and reliant on each other.

Many of these tools also have good export functionality, meaning that your information and data can be pulled out and used on other platforms, and so there is no need to be tied to just one platform. The constant change in the technological landscape can be frustrating and disorientating for many academics, and altmetrics is just part of that shift. LIS professionals can help their colleagues to understand the reasons for engaging with these technologies, defuse their concerns and provide solutions. This is an area in which they are very skilled, whether it be through the adoption of e-books, new databases or catalogues and technologies.

PART 2 STAYING ON TRACK

Academics are used to focusing on single problems or projects for prolonged periods. They become experts in their field by working in this way, and with the support of LIS professionals they can take advantage of altmetrics and social media in a way that should not affect their ways of working. While getting academics to first investigate and engage with new technologies can be a challenge, it can also have rewards. The embedded academic librarian can be helped in this by building professional relationships with other allied professions such as learning technologists, research support staff, IT and marketing professionals. Encouraging academics to stay on track with newly found technologies can be hard; they can be concerned that they don't have the time; and often they can feel alone in using a technology and be left wondering about the benefits when these have not yet been reaped. Encouraging academics to change how they work by using technology can have varied results, but the more positive outcomes happen when the LIS professional is visible as a means of support. Otherwise just one or two bad experiences, failures or disappointments can unravel the earlier work of gaining a researcher's trust to use the technology. Below are some strategies that LIS professionals can use to help academics stay on track once they start using altmetrics.

Find a twin

This is similar to the buddy system, which is often used to create a support network between two people who are working towards the same goal. Finding a twin involves seeking out someone whom you regard as a professional equal, whether in your job, department or grade, or with the same research interests. In order to win over the more sceptical users, the LIS professional can try to find a twin, someone the academic can genuinely relate to and, in particular, respect. This is very different to finding champions, where you look at your own organization for natural allies to champion change – often a researcher who carries much influence, career or personality-wise. Twins can include peers from outside the campus, or even from another country. Finding a twin can take time and research, and sometimes it is just as well to ask the reluctant academic who their peers are. It is likely that they will name one or two who are active on the social web, sharing references, presentations and publicly chatting about their research. Given that some senior academics are highly competitive, there is always a chance that they will view their peers being connected this way, and having a certain number of followers and an audience, as a challenge. Champions help the LIS professional to push the message across campus, but twins help to spur on (often without knowing it) a peer to engage more with altmetric technology. This will work only by showcasing academics to whom they can directly relate. It is unlikely that you would be able to encourage a professor of health economics to use Twitter by showing them how many followers and tweets a professor of history has. In our Information Resources department at the University of Sheffield we have used this tactic for many years with moderate success. The idea of using the term 'twin' was created by Claire Beecroft, the author of Chapter 10 in this book, who is herself a twin in real life.

Understand the researcher

Understanding researchers is something that cannot be overstated as a means to successful engagement. Academics come with all sorts of different personalities and agendas, and some are more approachable than others. There is no hard or fast rule; there are some professors whom you can approach comfortably, and some junior researchers whom you cannot. Nevertheless it is in the interests of the LIS professional to understand how the modern academic works, especially as this has changed dramatically since the advent of Web 2.0, mostly thanks to technology. Just think about how technology has impacted on every aspect of our lives – social media, e-mail, smartphones and cameras have changed hugely how we work, communicate and think. The modern academic's workflow is very different from what it would have been a generation ago. In the 1990s, there was very little access to the web and e-mail, mobile phones were the size of bricks and you had to take your camera film to a chemist in order to see the results of your holiday snaps. These things had little impact on academics and the way they worked; they wrote papers, read journals and books, gave lectures, attended conferences and meetings. They still do all of this and, as for the rest of the modern world, their workflow now has the potential to become incredibly fractured and distracted. The reason for this is simple: we are only ever a click away from the latest news, updates from friends, funny videos of cats and purchasing goods online. That is not to say academics are necessarily affected by this, but the development of Web 2.0 has opened up opportunities for distraction, and the social web has increased this incredibly. In the case of altmetrics and its close association with social networks and media it is important for any support and outreach to be delivered in a way that takes this into account. This is why it is crucial for LIS professionals trying to deliver new ideas and ways of working to understand not only what their users want but also how they work. The introduction of altmetrics into an academic community can be a disrupter (one that, it can be argued, is well overdue) and it may be met with varying degrees of enthusiasm. Also, taking into consideration technological change to support teaching and communication, it is important to remember that academics have had their workflows disrupted already. Consider that many now use virtual learning environments (VLEs), Google Apps, web conferencing and other technology systems for uploading their research and applying for funding; and this before we consider that e-mail has left many feeling overwhelmed by information overload. We also have to consider how such things as working online have led to ethical and technical questions over privacy, copyright and security. Remember that we now are talking about encouraging academics to become more visible on the web. There will be some who are highly sceptical about this change and will have concerns about what they can say, share and reply to. It is therefore crucial for LIS professionals to appear as allies and supporters, not burdens, and the best way to do that is to understand what their users want and how they work.

Knowing what users want and how they work is tacit knowledge that the LIS professional gains while in an organization. It becomes easier as you make contacts and build relationships to see who appreciates your support and looks for change, and who is happy to carry on as they are. The academics of the future will be very different from those of today. Their experiences as students, mostly influenced by technology, will be hugely different from those of their senior colleagues. We are now seeing a new generation of web users who engage with the web in a more immersed and fluid way than in the past and some of them will go on to become academics who, in turn, will be more likely to embed Web 2.0 and social media into their workflows.

You may already have made useful contacts with academics in your organization and have a good understanding of how they work and the pressures they face. If not, then a good approach for any LIS professional wanting to understand the modern researcher and how they work is to ask whether you can shadow them or undertake a survey of their perceptions of technology such as social media and altmetrics.

Make a good start

As previously noted, many of the altmetrics tools fall within the boundaries of both professional and personal use. It is a fair assumption that some academics are already comfortable using them, or at least believe themselves to be. However, that may be on a personal level, in a personal setting and at times when they are away from work and they may feel more liberal about what they say and share. Because social media is now well established and so many people now use it we tend to think that we know how to handle it. That said, the purpose of this book is not to explain how to use social media, but to explain how it can be applied fluently within an academic setting, why it matters and what the pitfalls are. One of the biggest problems is that social media reflects life – both the good and the bad – and that can extend to the workplace.

For academics to continue to engage with altmetrics they need a positive and beneficial experience from on the start. Using technology – especially social technology – for the first time can be a bit like going to a restaurant someone has recommended and not having an enjoyable experience. It is quite likely that one will never go back, and technology can be like that for some users, in that they try something new, have problems and decide not to use it again, or at least not for some time. A good example of this is when teaching staff accept students as Facebook friends, only to regret it later when they see it comprising their personal–professional boundaries. This can put them off using social technology.

Another problem is the very open and informal nature of social media. Academics can be put off by this openness and by the fact that others can use social media channels to direct criticism and even abuse towards them. There is the common problem that these tools can take time to proliferate and time to master, especially if the academic is on a steep technology learning curve. Take the example of an established career researcher who is moderately well known within their area of work. They may decide to start sharing their research and knowledge via Twitter. They may be aware that a few of their peers have been doing this for some time and have gained a good following from colleagues in the same field. The academic new to Twitter may expect to gain similar results fairly quickly and with minimal effort. Yet for most academics it takes some effort on their part, and they are more likely to be followed and retweeted if they tweet something that interests their peers. Once the academic finally launches their professional social profile there is another issue relating back to the issue of professional and personal boundaries. Even though many academics use tools like Twitter on a wholly professional level, others may want to show a personal and informal side of themselves. This can be off-putting for some fellow academics who would prefer just to know about their peer's research outputs rather than about what they had for breakfast.

Despite some users trying to lay down ground rules for social media use in academia, it really does come down to personal taste. Whether or not an academic is using social media and altmetrics correctly will come down to a few basic identifiers. First, have they gained an audience, and is it the right audience? If the academic is to engage with social media for their research they will need to reach the right people, with the same or similar research interests, whether they be journal editors, fundholders, academics, journalists or public servants. It is fine to have others following from outside these groups, but if the academic works in medicine and all of their followers are from the arts and humanities the chances are that they will not talk about medical research via these channels. As a result, there will be less chance of their content being shared to the right communities, and any metrics used, such as altmetrics, could reflect that later on.

Use your networks

It is important for academics stepping into the world of altmetrics and social media for scholarly communication and measurement to be given as much support as possible. And this support, where possible, does not have to come from LIS professional alone. Academic support staff often work either in isolation or as part of busy teams, and trying to get a group of academics to become socially and technologically adept can take up a lot of resources. This is where established networks and newly created ones can help. Often LIS professionals, especially the more social and technology-enabled ones, network and collaborate with other academic and professional groups. Through this networking they acquire further knowledge and techniques for enabling and helping others. In some institutions and organizations there will be a community of like-minded individuals who share knowledge and champion change, while others will operate in silos, doing great work but unaware of their colleagues' efforts. By being part of a network of like-minded peers from information and learning technology, libraries, marketing, communications and proactive academics already using social media and altmetrics, the LIS professional has a better chance of success. The secret of successful altmetrics adoption is to provide a consistent and helpful support base.

Find champions

Another approach that LIS professionals can take to encourage academics to engage with altmetrics is to discover and connect with those already engaging successfully with altmetrics tools within their organization. If the environment of the academic institution is just right, in that there are few barriers preventing users from engaging with technology, there is a good chance that there will already be technology champions on campus. These champions may already have worked with the support of professionals such as librarians, learning technologists and IT staff, or on their own initiative. Working with champions can have multiple benefits, first to share knowledge, resources and ideas; second to provide support to a user who may be open to receiving additional help; and third – the bonus – to help champion the library's cause. Champions can be very beneficial when you are trying to support an academic who is new to altmetrics, as they may be more receptive to change if it is underpinned by evidence from a colleague – especially a respected and proactive one.

Practise what you preach

For a librarian to have even greater success in encouraging academics to engage with altmetrics there is one simple rule that you must try to follow at all times. That is simply to practise what you preach. If you are instructing a student in how to use a software package to manage references, you should also use a software package to manage your references; and if you are instructing them in how to use altmetrics to promote and measure their research, you should use altmetrics in the same way wherever possible. Given that many LIS professionals work with technologies and web tools that are allied with altmetrics, that should not be difficult. For academics to understand and use altmetrics better, they need understanding, guidelines and continued support. As many LIS professionals have strong networks, attend conferences, seminars, webinars, workshops and committees, write papers, books and reports, give presentations and talks, and write blogs, among many other things, there is no shortage of content that they can broadcast to expert communities both synchronously and asynchronously. There are many quick wins to be had if the opportunities are taken and there will be a three-fold return of promoting your expertise, building networks and gaining skills to help academics to do the same.

Stay on focused on your topics

Another way for the modern LIS professional to engage with altmetrics and associated technologies is to try to stay up to date with new developments, discussions and ideas. This can come from Twitter and RSS feeds, following altmetrics, bibliometrics and academic blogs, and joining Mendeley, LinkedIn and ResearchGate groups. Curation tools like Pinterest, Evernote, Readability, Scoop.it! and Padlet can all be used to build evidence-based resources and hot-topic lists. This can be quite overwhelming, so it is important to use tools that can create digests and streamline content for you. It is also important to resist the desire to read everything on a given topic. Even in a subject like altmetrics, it is highly unlikely that you will be able to read everything published on the topic.

Raise awareness

Time is increasingly a problem for any professional who supports a wide user base, especially a proactive one who may work largely in isolation. Many reading this book will fit into this category and will spend large periods of their time working in isolation, perhaps attached to a group or team. Therefore it is important to follow the suggestions covered above, as they all form part of a strategy for supporting colleagues. For liaison librarians, information specialists and academic support professionals it can be very difficult to encourage academics with busy workflows to maximize their outputs and use different methods to measure them. Academics may not always appreciate the diverse skillsets that LIS professionals have; they may associate you with a library, books, databases and possibly how to review literature. The academics whom you support will probably all have different ideas of what your job entails; they will know either a large part or very little of what you can do to help them. Yet LIS professionals can have a wide range of skills, including teaching, training, appraisal, academic and blog writing, technical ability, communication and problem-solving, all of which can be applied to altmetrics.

Even with a wide set of skills and a potentially diverse set of users to support, there are still issues of how best to apply your time to creating awareness initiatives. These strategies are not exclusive to altmetrics training and promotion, and are good approaches to employ when encouraging academics to assess and understand this and all other technologies. Also, given that LIS professionals can receive a large number of enquiries on a daily basis, it is good practice to build processes that avoid duplication and repetition, where possible. There are several ways in which LIS professionals can use awareness sessions to help academics to better understand altmetrics and its associated technologies.

Instructional materials

Instructional materials can be delivered in many formats and have various pros and cons that are highlighted below.

Paper technology guides

Creating something as simple as a one-page instructional guide can be an effective way to help academics and others to understand the complexities of a technology, by providing an abstract of what it does and a list of its possible uses. By adding QR codes to web resources and videos you can help users to explore the technology further.

Pros: A quick and simple way of explaining a technology to a user without excessive cost in terms of time and production. Guides can be hosted online for users to download and read on a variety of platforms.

Cons: Technologies change fast, and paper guides will require updating on an 'as and when' basis. The more technology guides you compile, the more work you will have to make sure that they stay relevant.

Video guides

There is no better way to explain to users how to use a technology than by showing them in practice. Users can feel very anxious when faced with a technological change, especially one that could have a large impact on how they work. A video can help to demystify what a technology does, highlight key features and provide practical tips on its use. Videos can be created in a multitude of settings, from screencasts to talking heads, and do not have to be epic works of cinematography in order to put across how a technology can be applied. As for the cost of producing videos, this can be fairly cheap, thanks to free screencasting and production tools such as Screencast-O-Matic and Windows Movie Maker. You can also use video cameras and your own smartphone or tablet. For the video to have a real impact it needs to be short, preferably between one and three minutes long, but that will depend on the topic. Some videos may need more time and become mini-lectures lasting up to 20 minutes. If this is the case, see whether you can 'chunk' the video into more manageable pieces. This has three practical advantages. First, it will allow you to drill down into the technology and explain a key feature. For example, it can take some time for users to fully understand how Twitter works and benefits the academic community. They may feel that Twitter is a tool used exclusively by celebrities and teenagers, which then becomes a barrier to its use. You could make a video that explains hashtags and their use within a conference or teaching setting, or for putting a question to a peer group. A second benefit of dividing your videos into chunks is that the information will be easier for users to digest and users will be able to view them at times that suit them. The third benefit is that, as with any kind of guide, the videos can go out of date and re-recording just part of a video will be much less time-consuming than recording the whole thing again.

The quality of the video and its level of detail will depend on what time and technology resources you have. The more complex the video, for example if you take multiple shots of yourself, and the more difficult the technology, the more time it will take to record and edit it. Nevertheless, this should not put you off, because videos have become a common and effective medium for library and information instruction.

Something else you will have to consider is the audio content. It is important for users to be able to hear clearly what you are saying, especially if the topic may be alien to them. Audio recording provides an option for LIS professionals who would prefer not to appear on screen. They can make screencasts of their desktops or record audio-only versions of tutorials, but only if they think the content would translate effectively to an audio guide.

Pros: An effective way to explain to users what a technology does and how they can use it. Video guides can be viewed on mobile devices and are a good way to build collections of learning tutorials. They help LIS professionals build their own technology skillset.

Cons: Can be time-consuming if making more complex videos and have a bigger learning curve if comprehensive video editing is needed. Videos can date very quickly for some topics or technologies, especially if a technology or tool changes every few months.

Workshops, awareness and bite-size sessions

LIS professionals often spend a lot of time supporting users on a one-to-one basis, which in time can be quite a drain on resources and time. It is important for any LIS professional or academic thinking of running awareness sessions to create them to suit a variety of situations.

A good way to engage with academics when talking about something like altmetrics is to offer bite-size or short awareness sessions. This will help to pique their interest but avoid overloading them with fresh content and ideas and making them commit to adopting the technology at the session. Anyone who has ever run a workshop that lasts for more than an hour or so can testify to the amount of time that can go into preparation. It is important for any altmetrics workshop to have a good structure and, if possible, a few objectives for participants to take away from it. There also need to be follow-ups if possible, which might take the form of short one-to-one sessions, e-mail enquiries to a point of contact or, better still, tweets. While it is important to note that altmetrics can be pitched at various levels, there is no need to jump in at the deep end. For example, to get academics interested, or at least to dip a toe in the water, it is better to start with shorter, informal workshops and seminars. One successful way to reach out to academics is to run a taster session that may last 20 minutes and to allow 10 minutes for questions. Short 'bite-size' sessions like this have the benefit of not requiring much time to prepare, and also not taking up much time for the busy academic. Try to run the session in an area of the campus that has a dense population of academics. Many academics are prepared to give up only so much time for a seminar or training session, especially if they are not so sure about the topic, and will not want to spend additional time travelling to it. If the session is informal, the LIS professional can be prepared for attendees to ask questions at any point, as well as to come late and go early, as they wish. In effect it is a no-pressure sales pitch that can be applied to any form of staff development. Sessions like this can be offered as continuing professional development points in some departments.

Running short, less formal sessions provides a good opportunity for capture by screencasting or video so that those who did not attend can watch the recording at a later date, knowing that they will not have to put aside a large chunk of their time in order to do so.

Pros: A good way to capture the attention of several academics at a time and for them to meet colleagues with similar interests. Saves duplication of effort and can be a way to meet academics and highlight the skills that you can offer. Many altmetrics tools are quick and easy to understand, so this is a good way to give academics a clear explanation of them in one go.

Cons: Can be disheartening when no one turns up. May leave academics with more questions than answers if not delivered right. Depending on complexity of topics and length of sessions, preparation can be considerable if you are trying to build a comprehensive workshop or seminar.

Conclusion

Throughout the course of any LIS professional's career they will face many challenges, tough questions, tasks and users – especially when it comes to trying to change practice. It is important always to keep in mind the individuals and groups that you support and to understand their cultures and beliefs. Altmetrics is part of a major shift within academia, perhaps one that may lead to that mythical paradigm shift we often hear about. Academics need to understand why they should engage with these technologies and tools, and their benefits, barriers and pitfalls.

Key points

- A one size-fits-all approach does not work when trying to implement technology or organizational change.
- Not all academics embrace technology; it is important to remember that everyone takes their own time when adapting to change.
- If librarians employ technology themselves to teach altmetrics and other innovations they can in turn improve their own skill sets.
- Academics and LIS professionals need to understand the differences between social media and altmetrics, and that the latter is not wholly reliant on the former for its data.
- LIS professionals need a good understanding of researchers and the research life cycle when advocating new technologies such as altmetrics.
- All new technology needs critical appraisal before adoption, especially when employing third-party tools.

Reference

Franklin, B. (2007) *The Autobiography of Benjamin Franklin (1706–1757)*, The Lakeside Press.

Web resource

Gartner Hype Cycle:
www.gartner.com/technology/research/methodologies/hype-cycle.jsp.

Further reading

Korn, N. with Oppenheim, C. (2017) *The No-Nonsense Guide to Licensing Digital Resources*, Facet Publishing, not yet published.

Notess, G. R. (2012) *Screencasting for Libraries*, Facet Publishing.

Peltier-Davis, C. A. (2012) *The Cybrarian's Web*, Facet Publishing.

Priem, J. (2010) I Like the Term #Articlelevelmetrics, But it Fails to Imply *Diversity* of Measures: lately, I'm liking #altmetrics, Twitter, 29 September, https://twitter.com/jasonpriem/status/25844968813 [accessed 11 July 2015].

Reed, L. and Signnorelli, P. (2011) *Workplace Learning and Leadership*, ALA Editions.

CHAPTER 10

Appmetrics: improving impact on the go

Claire Beecroft

Introduction

Mobile 'smart' devices have increased greatly in popularity since Apple's first iPhone, with 61% of UK adults now owning a smartphone (Ofcom, 2014). The emergence of the tablet computer has added significantly to the utilities available via mobile devices, and the adoption of mobile technologies for work-related activities is ever expanding. However, relatively few academic staff who use these devices make full use of the range of options available, and many lack awareness of the apps they could be using to promote their outputs and improve impact on the go. Information professionals need to stay abreast of current and emerging developments in mobile apps in order to support academic staff in using their mobile devices effectively to improve and monitor their research impact.

There are many apps and tools to choose from. This chapter looks at an essential 'toolkit' of apps that information professionals should bear in mind when supporting and advising academic staff on research impact, and gives advice on how to make the best and most efficient use of them. Additionally, the chapter will examine how impact activities undertaken on a mobile device can be fitted into a flexible working day.

Glossary

The following are some key terms that I will use frequently throughout the chapter, and their definitions.

Android – an operating system developed by Google for use on smartphones and tablets. There is a very wide choice of devices, at varied price points. Updated regularly.

Blackberry OS – the operating system used by Blackberry smart devices. Declining in popularity in recent years, but still quite widely used by business people and in countries such as India.

iOS – the operating system developed for Apple mobile devices. Only iPhones and iPads run iOS. Updated regularly.

OS – acronym for operating system. The most popular ones for mobile devices are iOS and Android, but there are also Windows Mobile and Blackberry, among others.

Smart device – any mobile computing device that can connect to the web via 3G/4G or WiFi. These include tablet computers such as iPads, smartphones and small-format laptops such as Netbooks and Chromebooks.

Windows Mobile – the operating system developed for Microsoft Windows mobile devices. There is a wider range of devices to choose from than with iOS, but fewer than with Android. Good for people who are familiar with Windows and would prefer to use a tablet with an easy-to-learn user interface that has been designed to integrate with Microsoft software, such as Microsoft Office.

How can mobile help?

Many academic staff now own a mobile device; most often this is a smartphone, but increasingly a tablet is becoming an essential piece of kit. While most of us make good use of our mobile devices for administrative tasks such as checking e-mail or our diary, many staff admit that they do not know how to maximize use and get the best value out of their mobile device. Equally, many academic staff say that they struggle to find the time to integrate impact-generating activity into an already busy work schedule. One of the key benefits of mobile technology is that it is always there, ready and waiting to help academic staff generate impact. This can be at any time when they have a few minutes to spare, or when inspiration strikes. Knowing how to get the best out of smart devices is vital for information professionals, as this knowledge, combined with specialist knowledge in an academic discipline, can help to position LIS professionals as key stakeholders in the 'brave new world' of altmetrics.

Previous chapters have looked at the academic value of social tools such as Twitter, but what difference does it make whether they are used on a desktop or on a mobile device? Two key factors in favour of mobile devices are their time and timeliness. Some key factors in favour of the mobile device are the following:

- Mobile devices often allow voice dictation. This enables the user to speak into the device and have their voice input converted to text. This can vastly improve the efficiency of tasks such as blogging, tweeting and communicating via social networks.
- Most mobile devices have the capacity to record decent-quality audio and video. Using these tools, it is possible to produce engaging content that can serve as an alternative to a traditional blog post and be completed with speed and efficiency.
- Mobile devices are carried by most of us, most of the time. Given the highly time-sensitive nature of networks such as Twitter, being able to use these networks adeptly on mobile devices can make the difference between being able to enter into and engage in conversations or 'missing the boat' as the tide of interest in a trending topic relevant to an academic's research interests ebbs away.

Which mobile device is best?

Academic staff may ask for advice on which mobile device would suit them best. While this is not an area on which LIS professionals should feel obliged to advise, they can help academic staff to make their own choice by suggesting that they think about the following issues.

What devices do your colleagues use?

It may be helpful to choose a device that other colleagues use, as it may make cross-team working and collaboration more fluid, and there is more likely to be in-house expertise, both formal and informal, to support them in using the device.

Which devices do you already own?

If someone is already using an Android phone, buying an Android tablet will facilitate a shallow learning curve. Equally, aiming for 'the best of both worlds' by having an Android phone and Apple tablet, or viceversa, can ensure that the fullest possible range of apps and functions is available.

Do you want to use voice input?

Both Android and iOS devices allow users to enter text and give commands via speech input, but iOS voice input, Siri, is arguably far superior, with higher precision when converting natural speech to text and adding grammar (Bellegarda, 2013). Using voice input can be a huge boost to productivity, so it is worth thinking about this when choosing a device.

What apps would you like to use?

Bear in mind that some apps are available on only one mobile platform, Turnitin and Adobe Voice being examples in academia of apps that are available via iOS, so it is important to be clear about which apps are important and which devices will provide access to them.

Can I borrow a device to try it?

Increasingly, library and information services are loaning mobile devices to academic staff and students (DeCesare, Posey and Bellotti, 2013). This can provide an ideal opportunity for academics to experiment with a mobile device so as to decide whether it would be worth the investment for them personally, and to assess how it would impact on their daily work activities.

Distraction, and how to deal with it

Fitting in activity on mobile devices can be incredibly useful. However, use of a mobile device can also lead to longer hours spent working, and work activities creeping into evenings and weekends. Lisa Donnelly notes that 'both organizations and some individuals have yet to establish acceptable boundaries in relation to the use of smartphones for work based activities outside of legal working hours' (Donnelly, 2011). Without formal guidance, it is up to the individual to take control of how they use mobile devices for work tasks, and to that end there are some tips and tricks that can help to ensure that academic staff do not find themselves spending more time than they wish to on work activities via their mobile device.

It is increasingly recognized that mobile devices and the web can present a major source of distraction to users during working hours and can be both barriers to and enhancers of productivity (Machado, Machado and Sousa, 2014). A device that is incessantly alerting its owner to the latest e-mail, tweet or social media 'mention' is not helpful. It is annoying and can end up costing more time that it saves.

The single most important step in managing apps is to ensure that notifications from apps are set to the user's preferences, not the app's own presets. When installing new apps, users often find that a message pops up asking if they would like to receive notifications. It is all too easy to routinely click 'yes', just to get past that step and gain access to the new app, but it is important to be sure that notifications are correctly set up. An app such as Twitter can easily send ten or more notifications a day even to a modest user, and so it is important that users decide what they want to be notified about, and how.

This can be done in two ways. First of all, when installing new apps, users should think before answering 'yes' to notifications – do they really want this app to send alerts? Second, for apps already installed, it should be possible to manage notifications via the device's 'settings' menu and get them set up so that they are helpful, not a hindrance.

How notifications work: an example

In Twitter, notifications can let a user know when a tweet they have sent has been favourited or retweeted. Alerts can inform the user when they have been mentioned in a tweet. They can also inform the user when a direct message is received that may need immediate attention. It's up to the user to decide whether they want to use Twitter notifications, but notifications can help by simply reminding the user to check their account regularly so as to keep on top of conversations and ensure that they don't miss anything important. Twitter is perhaps the most timebound of the apps examined in this chapter, and keeping up to date at certain key times can be important, particularly if a user's research is featured in mass media or related to a current news story. For this reason users may need to switch notifications on or off at different times.

What apps can help academic staff to improve their research impact?

Research impact itself is difficult to define. The traditional metrics, such as citation rates, have been used by the Higher Education Funding Council for England (HEFCE) in England to measure impact, and, while they are debatable, they are clearly still very important. One of the simplest ways an academic can improve their citation rate is by using academic social networks and Twitter to promote published research. A consideration here is the availability of their research via open access and how easily the research can be viewed on a mobile device. For example, users may complain if a tweeted link to a research paper leads them to a pay wall, or to content in a format that their device cannot display. These considerations aside, however, this is a simple and very effective way of increasing the readership of research. When attempting to increase research impact it may be important to reach not just the researcher's peers, but organizations, policy makers and the general public, to name but a few. The traditional approach of assuming that once research is published it will be found by those who could use it is optimistic at best. Mobile devices offer users numerous opportunities to play an active role in generating impact for their research beyond the conventional measures outlined above, using their own words to explain and communicate their research on their own terms, and enable them to tailor their messages to a specific audience for maximum impact. Prices of apps are correct at time of going to press.

The Altmetrics Mobile Toolkit

While it is difficult to identify the 'must-have' apps for academics who are looking to increase impact, the apps and app-genres listed below could provide a good starting point. Many are free, but those that are charged for are identified and prices at the time of writing are given. Please bear in mind that the app market is highly volatile, with apps appearing and disappearing constantly, so the aim here is to give LIS professionals an idea of the types of apps and their functionality and how they can improve research impact (or help users to monitor impact), rather than to focus closely on specific 'recommended' apps. It is up to individuals to choose what works for them, but LIS professionals can guide users as to which apps might be worth investigating from an impact perspective.

Video editing apps, e.g. iMovie (£3.99 iOS), AndroVid (£1.69 or free with ads, Android), KineMaster (£2.91 per month, £23.25 annually, or free with watermark on videos, Android)

Communicating research is not an activity that many researchers have engaged with, outside of publishing and speaking at conferences. However, in a world where the value of research is increasingly measured by its impact rather than by readership and citation rates, the agile researcher needs to break out of the academic world and take their research directly to those who can benefit from it. Video is a particularly powerful tool for achieving this aim.

A key use for video is for academics to talk about their published research, either in lay terms for general consumption or by addressing researchers and clinicians in a brief, accessible way and outside the constraints of the traditional background–methods–results format of scholarly journals. This allows them to express their personality, explain their work in their own terms, and focus on the key messages they would like to get across about the potential impact of their research and how it might be used. How others use and share your video will depend on what they hope to achieve, but the next two examples are key mobile apps for viewing video.

YouTube (free on iOS and Android, often pre-installed on Android devices)

The world's most popular and best-known video hosting and sharing platform, YouTube is a great place to upload videos if the key aim is to reach the widest possible audience. There are risks in doing this, as the platform is also awash with videos of surfing cats and skateboarding dogs, and it is inevitable that academics may feel uncomfortable about sharing their content on such a platform; but YouTube is highly flexible and users can embed YouTube videos into a range of other websites without having to make them 'findable' on the YouTube site itself. It is also worth bearing in mind the increasing use of YouTube as a news source, recent research showing that journalists are increasingly engaging with news-related content on the platform: 'news organizations are taking advantage of citizen content and incorporating it into their journalism' (Pew Research Center, 2012).Therefore, posting videos to YouTube may help to get information about research into the wider media. There are limits on the length of videos that can be posted from a personal YouTube account, but, given the relatively short attention span of the modern web user, YouTube's standard ten-minute limit should give most academics plenty of time to get their key points and ideas across effectively and concisely. Most smart devices now allow users to upload videos directly from the device to YouTube, making it a good option for times when one needs to get a video shot, edited and published quickly and on the go.

Vimeo (free on iOS and Android)

Less well known than YouTube, Vimeo has many of the same characteristics: it allows users to create an account where they can upload videos and share and embed them across the web. Vimeo differs from YouTube in that it does not limit the length of each video, but instead limits the amount of data that a user can upload each month. This means that Vimeo may be an ideal tool for longer videos than YouTube will allow. It also attracts more professionally produced content, so there are fewer skateboarding dogs, and some academics may feel that their content simply fits into the Vimeo environment better. The Vimeo app for Android and iOS devices allows users to upload video directly to Vimeo from a mobile device.

Traditionally, recording and editing video required a substantial investment in equipment and a steep learning curve. However, most of us carry a video camera in our pocket, thanks to smartphones, and editing to a decent quality is astonishingly easy with the modest investment of £3 to £7 in a good-quality video-editing app. There are numerous options, but the Apple iMovie app is a good example of a simple editing interface that can be learned quickly and can enable even a novice to turn a simple 'talking head' video into something smart enough for wide circulation online and via social networks. For Android devices, AndroVid offers basic editing and exporting, and KineMaster Pro gives a full-featured editor, but with an ongoing cost.

How can LIS professionals support the use of these apps?

LIS professionals are in a strong position to advise on the suitability of the different video platforms, and on the crucial issues of copyright and intellectual property relating to the content contained in videos. Academics need advice on the use of images, tables and multimedia content within videos, on how to enable appropriate access to video content, and on using privacy and security restrictions to ensure that content is available only to the desired audiences. Similarly, academics may need advice on how to ensure that further sharing of their video content by viewers is set to their own preferences rather than to the default settings of the video platform.

Audio-recording apps, e.g. audioBoom (free for both iOS and Android), Voice Record Pro (free or £2.29 without adverts on iOS), Voice Recorder (free on Android but with in-app purchase of some features)

An important but often overlooked approach to achieving greater impact with research is to reach a wider audience than is possible via scholarly journals, even those available via open access. There are many means of doing this, one of which is to investigate alternative multimedia formats, including audio.

For staff who would prefer to keep their audio content offline, or simply to have a little more control over how it is used and shared, there is an array of simple voice-recording apps that allow users to record some audio and download it from their device to a computer in a variety of common audio formats including .wav and .mp4. Voice Record Pro for iOS and Voice Recorder for Android are two examples of such apps. They are easy to use and allow unlimited recording time.

How can LIS professionals support the use of these apps?

Many academic library environments now incorporate multimedia editing resources and LIS professionals can use appmetrics activities as a way of marketing and promoting these resources and obtaining any support that is available in using them. As with video, LIS professionals may also be able to provide advice on audio-content copyright issues and on setting up restrictions on the sharing of audio recordings that are made available online.

Twitter-monitoring tools: Hootsuite (free for iOS and Android), TweetDeck (no app, optimizes for mobile devices)

There are several tools that can be used to monitor Twitter and other social media platforms from a mobile device, the best-known being TweetDeck and Hootsuite. These can be particularly useful for academics when attending conferences, particularly if they are presenting their own research while there. Tools such as these enable users to monitor multiple Twitter accounts and multiple Twitter hashtags and conversations simultaneously from a single screen. This can be immensely useful when monitoring conference hashtags or maintaining Twitter conversations with conference attendees, enabling users to maximize the opportunity to promote their research. They are best used on tablet devices, because of the amount of data displayed.

How can LIS professionals support the use of these apps?

By 2011, Mahmood and Richardson found that there was 'overwhelming acceptance of various Web 2.0 tools in large academic libraries' (Mahmood and Richardson, 2011). As early adopters of social media tools, including Twitter, many LIS professionals are ahead of their academic colleagues in their experience and knowledge of social media management tools. Tools such as Hootsuite may seem confusing at first, as they display multiple feeds of data, and learning how to set up and monitor these streams beneficially is vital. Del Bosque, Lief and Skari (2012) note that 'libraries understand the power of Twitter as a practical channel of communication', but academic staff may still struggle both to see its value and to see how it can be used efficiently and productively. LIS professionals can offer support sessions on the use of these tools, and also highlight the opportunity that they offer to bridge the online and offline worlds by allowing users to make online contacts via Twitter that lead to face-to-face networking.

Reading apps, e.g. Pocket, Readability, Evernote Web Clipper (free for iOS and Android)

More and more research is finding its way online via formats such as news articles, blog posts and 'plain language' summaries. Reading online can be a strain and highly distracting, as pop-up ads and banners vie for users' attention and attempt to drag them away from an article and onto a commercial site. Reading apps such as Pocket (formerly 'Read it Later') and Readability help by allowing users to store online articles for reading now or later and stripping out all but the text-based content, ensuring a 'clean' and simple reading experience with no distractions. Evernote Web Clipper is a feature of the Evernote app; it allows users to 'clip' copies of web-based content to add to their Evernote library for later, offline reading. Web Clipper can be enabled within the Evernote app.

Reading is a vital part of the research process, so making reading on a mobile device a viable option is important for academics who want to fill their commuting time with useful activity.

How can LIS professionals support the use of these apps?

Successful use of reading apps relies on proper organization and tagging of saved content to facilitate easy identification and retrieval at a later date; these are skills that are inherent to most LIS professionals. Providing support to academic staff on properly tagging or keywording saved resources could be very useful. This skill is also transferable to the use of reference management tools, which similarly rely on efficient tagging and categorizing of uploaded references

Reference management apps, e.g. Mendeley (free on Android and iOS), EndNote (£2.49 for iOS, not available for Android)

Mendeley is best known as an online reference management tool, but its mobile application allows users to access their library references on the go, and also to search and discover via the vast Mendeley database, comprising the Mendeley libraries of millions of Mendeley users. It is an excellent multidisciplinary discovery tool that is highly accessible when on the go. Many of the current altmetric measurement tools, including Altmetric.com and Impactstory, are able to harvest data from the Mendeley database, so being an active user of this resource and ensuring that all their research papers are in the Mendeley database is an important first step for academics who wish to improve the impact of their research.

How can LIS professionals support the use of these apps?

Support on the use of reference management tools is commonly provided by academic library services, so support on the use of apps related to reference management could be incorporated into existing services and sessions.

Tagging or keywording references is a vital skill that can assist academic staff more generally in their use of information.

News apps, e.g. reddit is fun (free on Android), Alien Blue for reddit (free on iOS), BBC News (free on iOS and Android), Reuters (free on iOS and Android)

News and current affairs apps are a staple of most people's smart devices, and they can be useful for identifying news stories in areas that relate to an academic's own research. While a topic is 'hot,' users can make use of the short-term attention on the topic area by blogging, tweeting (using any relevant hashtags that are trending) or writing for websites such as The Conversation. These require academics to be quick and reactive, so a good news app is helpful to ensure that they don't miss a relevant story. The BBC News app has a highly customizable interface, with very detailed topic areas, allowing users to focus the app on just those areas of news that are most relevant to their research. For example, as well as typically broad news categories such as 'technology', there are sub-topics for 'mobile phones', 'tablets', 'apps' and 'cybersecurity'. Selecting only the most relevant topics can make news apps more useful and less distracting. The Reuters app is highly international and vast in its content, but the key categories are quite broad. However, the search function allows users to find content effectively and the editorial quality is high. Alien Blue is an iOS app giving access to the news/reading service reddit, which allows members to post content such as links to news stories and other web content, and to comment on it. Reddit ranks users' posts by allowing users to 'vote' them 'up' or 'down'. There are a myriad topic areas within the site that users can explore – some are admittedly fairly 'light', but there are also plenty of intelligent posts, comment and debate around topics rooted in academic research. The site can give a sense of what users are discussing in relation to a story and how it is influencing opinion – something worth looking at by academics who are trying to gain more media exposure for their research. Android users could try 'reddit is fun', a similar app for reddit.

How can LIS professionals support the use of these apps?

A vital skill in using news-related apps is being able to search for and identify relevant articles quickly and efficiently. LIS professionals are well placed to offer advice on using appropriate search terms to identify articles, and also to use their current-awareness skills to help academics set up automated alerts so that they are regularly updated on the latest relevant stories as soon as they become available.

Altmetrics tool apps, e.g.Impactstory, Altmetrics, Academia.edu, ResearchGate

These specific altmetrics tools are discussed in more detail elsewhere in this book, but there are some good reasons to access them via a mobile device:

- Having a direct link to key altmetrics tools will make academics more likely to check them regularly, allowing them to keep up with how their work is being read, shared, cited and used.

- It is often possible to use a mobile device to add content to a personal account on many altmetrics tools, uploading documents, spreadsheets, slides and posters direct from Google Drive, Dropbox, Evernote, OneDrive etc. Small tasks like this, which might be distracting during the working day, may be more easily completed during a commute or when working from home.
- These tools have a strong social element, allowing researchers to communicate with each other and share data and other resources. As we have seen above, use of social platforms is increasingly a natural activity on mobile devices, and integrating work-related social networking on a mobile device could be equally so.
- Altmetrics is a highly reactive medium, and using a mobile device is a natural way to harness the immediacy of feedback and conversations that can occur as soon as a research article, or other research output, is published. This may occur outside conventional working hours, and so using a mobile device is an ideal way to engage, for instance while commuting.
- Academics who have a Google Scholar profile can adjust the settings within their profile to send alerts to e-mail. They can then set up their e-mail to alert them when e-mails from .scholar.google.com arrive, giving an early indication each time their work is cited, and a chance to take a look at the work that has cited their own.

While many altmetrics sites and tools may be browser based, with no companion app, academics can still make better use of them on a mobile device by creating shortcuts to them and giving prominence to them on their mobile device's home screen. These shortcuts can be grouped according to the user's research interests. Creating shortcuts is simple on most smart devices, and instructions for the top three mobile browsers are given below:

Chrome (Google's web browser and operating system): Tap the three vertical dots in the top right-hand corner, then tap 'add to home screen'.

Safari (Apple's web browser): Tap the box with the upward-pointing arrow in the top right-hand corner, then tap 'add to home screen'.

Firefox on Android: Tap the 'recents' or 'task switcher' key on the device (the one on the navigation bar at the bottom of your device that has either three stacked lines or two stacked rectangles), then choose 'page' and 'add to home screen'.

Bear in mind that monitoring citations and mentions of research can easily become addictive, so it is important not to encourage academics to become overly engaged with citation rates and stats, but simply to use them to monitor the impact of their overall impact activities on their citation rates and online mentions or shares. This can give academics a sense of reward for their efforts, and also help to identify which tools are working best for them and which they might choose to discontinue using.

How can LIS professionals support the use of these apps?

Here a key role for LIS professionals is to support academic staff in choosing the most relevant altmetrics tools to help them achieve their impact goals and, in particular, to identify those that are worth monitoring and interacting with regularly via a mobile device. LIS professionals can also advise academics on setting up their profiles on altmetrics sites and on ensuring that they have a complete and up-to-date profile at all times that reflects their current research output and interests.

Conclusion: making appmetrics a part of the daily routine

As we have seen, there are a range of apps and tools that can be used on mobile devices to enable academics to maximize their research impact on the go. While information overload is a common problem in modern life, when used wisely these apps and tools can help to ensure that academics make effective use of their time and improve their online profile and impact.

Finding the tools that work best for an individual is, to a certain extent, a matter of trial and error, but LIS professionals are well placed to offer support and guidance, combining their specialist subject knowledge and understanding of altmetrics, reference management, social media, copyright and keywording and tagging data to help academic staff make their apps work hard to maximize research impact and minimize time and effort.

Key points

- Altmetrics requires academics to increase their engagement with social media and to produce new forms of content that can be shared online to improve scholarly communication and impact.
- Using mobile apps allows academics to undertake key altmetrics activities and to fit them around their existing workload.
- LIS professionals are well placed to support academics in their use of these apps, drawing on their skills in digital literacy, searching, keywording, social media and copyright.
- Many academic libraries could incorporate support for apps into existing information literacy activities and use support for apps as a vehicle for promoting library services and facilities, such as media-editing facilities.
- Supporting the use of apps can also help to position LIS professionals and academic libraries at the forefront of altmetrics, demonstrating the unique skills and value that they bring to academic institutions.

References

Bellegarda, J. (2013) Spoken Language Understanding for Natural Interaction: the siri experience. In *Natural Interaction with Robots, Knowbots and Smartphones*, Springer, 3–14.

DeCesare, J. A., Posey, H. and Bellotti, C. (2013) Lending iPads 101: steps to loan from your library. In *NERCOMP Annual Conference/EDUCAUSE, Providence, RI, March 2013*, http://works.bepress.com/hailie_posey/7.

Del Bosque, D., Lief, S. A. and Skari, S. (2012) Libraries Atwitter: trends in academic library tweeting, *Reference Services Review*, **40** (2), www.emeraldinsight.com/doi/full/10.1108/.

Donnelly, L. (2011) *The effect of Smartphones on Work-life Balance*, www.academia.edu/2074574/The_effect_of_Smartphones_on_work_life_balance.

Machado, C. F., Machado, J. C. and Sousa, M. C. (2014) Human Resource Management and the Internet: challenge and/or threat to workplace productivity? In *Human Resource Management and Technological Challenges*,

Springer International Publishing, 149–68.

Mahmood, K. and Richardson, J. V. Jr (2011) Adoption of Web 2.0 in US
Academic Libraries: a survey of ARL library websites, *Program*, **45** (4),
www.emeraldinsight.com/doi/full/10.1108/.

Ofcom (2014) *The Communications Market Report: United Kingdom*,
http://stakeholders.ofcom.org.uk/market-data-research/
market-data/communications-market-reports/cmr14/uk.

Pew Research Center (2012) *YouTube & News*, Pew Research Center's
Journalism Project, www.journalism.org/2012/07/16/youtube-news/.

Web resources

Alien Blue for iOS: https://itunes.apple.com/gb/app/alien-blue-reddit-official/
id923187241?mt=8.

AndroVid:
https://play.google.com/store/apps/details?id=com.androvid&hl=en_GB.

audioboom for Android:
https://play.google.com/store/apps/details?id=com.audioboom&hl=en_GB.

audioboom for iOS:
https://itunes.apple.com/gb/app/audioboom/id305204540?mt=8.

BBC News for Android:
https://play.google.com/store/apps/details?id=bbc.mobile.news.uk&hl=en.

BBC News for Blackberry:
https://appworld.blackberry.com/webstore/content/13859/?lang=en.

BBC News for iOS:
https://itunes.apple.com/gb/app/bbc-news/id377382255?mt=8.

BBC News for Windows Mobile:
https://www.microsoft.com/en-gb/store/apps/bbc-news/9nblggh08q4r.

EndNote for iOS: https://itunes.apple.com/gb/app/endnote-for-ipad/
id593994211?mt=8.

Evernote for Android:
https://play.google.com/store/apps/details?id=com.evernote&hl=en_GB.

Evernote for iOS:
https://itunes.apple.com/gb/app/evernote/id281796108?mt=8.

Evernote for Windows Mobile: https://www.microsoft.com/en-gb/store/
apps/evernote/9wzdncrfj3n1.

Hootsuite for Android: https://play.google.com/store/apps/

details?id=com.hootsuite.droid.full&hl=en_GB.

Hootsuite for iOS: https://itunes.apple.com/gb/app/hootsuite-schedule-posts-for/id341249709?mt=8.

iMovie: https://itunes.apple.com/gb/app/imovie/id377298193?mt=8

KineMaster: https://play.google.com/store/apps/details?id=com.nexstreaming.app.kinemasterfree&hl=en_GB.

Mendeley for Android:
https://play.google.com/store/apps/details?id=com.mendeley&hl=en_GB.

Mendeley for iOS: https://itunes.apple.com/gb/app/mendeley-pdf-reader/id380669300?mt=8.

Pocket for Android: https://play.google.com/store/apps/details?id=com.ideashower.readitlater.pro&hl=en_GBPocket for iOS: https://itunes.apple.com/gb/app/pocket-save-articles-videos/id309601447?mt=8.

Readability for Android:
https://play.google.com/store/apps/details?id=com.readability&hl=en_GB.

Readability for iOS:
https://itunes.apple.com/gb/app/readability/id460156587?mt=8.

Reddit is fun:
https://play.google.com/store/apps/details?id=com.andrewshu.android.reddit&hl=en_GB.

Reddit is fun for Android: https://play.google.com/store/apps/details?id=com.andrewshu.android.reddit&hl=en_GB.

Reuters for Android: https://play.google.com/store/apps/details?id=com.thomsonreuters.reuters&hl=en.

Reuters for iOS: https://itunes.apple.com/gb/app/reuters/id602660809?mt=8.

Vimeo for Android:
https://play.google.com/store/apps/details?id=com.vimeo.android.videoapp&hl=en_GB.

Vimeo for iOS: https://itunes.apple.com/gb/app/vimeo/id425194759?mt=8.

Vimeo for Windows Mobile: https://www.microsoft.com/en-us/store/apps/vimeo/9wzdncrfj2ms.

Voice Record Pro iOS: https://itunes.apple.com/gb/app/voice-record-pro/id546983235?mt=8.

Voice Recorder Android: https://play.google.com/store/apps/details?id=com.splendapps.voicerec&hl=en_GB.

YouTube for Android: https://play.google.com/store/apps/details?id=com.google.android.youtube&hl=en_GB.

YouTube for iOS:
   https://itunes.apple.com/gb/app/youtube/id544007664?mt=8.
YouTube for Windows Mobile: https://www.microsoft.com/en-
   us/store/apps/youtube/9wzdncrfj3dl.

Further reading

Canuel, R. and Crichton, C. (2016) Leveraging Apps for Research and
   Learning: a survey of Canadian academic libraries, *Library Hi Tech*, **33** (1),
   2–14, www.emeraldinsight.com/doi/full/10.1108/LHT-12–2014-0115.

Hoffmann, M. (2015) An Exploratory Study: mobile device use for academics
   (Order No. 3685662), ProQuest Dissertations and Theses A&I (1664843577),
   http://search.proquest.com/docview/1664843577?accountid=13828.

Knoblauch, H. and Knoblauch, H. (2013) *Smartphone Cameras and Academic
   Research, JustPublics@365*, https://justpublics365.commons.gc.cuny.edu/06/
   2013/smart-phones-and-academic-research/.

Libguides.mit.edu (2016) Library Research – Apps for Academics: mobile web
   sites and apps – Libguides at MIT Libraries,
   http://libguides.mit.edu/c.php?g=176092&p=1158704.

Sclafani, J., Tirrell, T. and Franko, O. (2013) Mobile Tablet Use among
   Academic Physicians and Trainees, *Journal of Medical Systems*, **37** (1), 9903,
   doi:10.1007/s10916-012-9903-6.

CHAPTER 11

Open peer review

Andy Tattersall

Introduction

The purpose of this chapter is to introduce readers to engagement by academics in open post-publication peer review of others' research. This is not new, but this book would not be complete without some discussion of this growing area of interest, given that its major focus is on scholarly communication and measurement. This chapter will be of particular interest to LIS professionals who are involved in open access and scholarly communication work. It will explain what open peer review is, in all its variations, and discuss and review some of the main protagonists in this area. The chapter will explain why open peer review (in particular, post publication) is gaining interest. It will also discuss some of the barriers and opportunities presented by the opening up of academic research.

Main body

The term 'peer review' is likely to send shudders down the spines of most researchers who have ever edited, reviewed or written a piece of research. Yet it is a necessary part of the research process and without it we would see every Tom, Dick or Harry publish their work to a potential audience. Even so, there is plenty of evidence that fraudulent publishing still occurs, despite peer review existing in its present form. Peer review is a way of making sure that a piece of research is of good quality, thorough and fit for dissemination in the publication in question. There are several models of peer review in research, the most common being single blind, where the reviewers know the identity of the author(s). There is also double-blind peer review, where neither the author(s) nor the reviewers know each other's identity. Open peer review is where one or both of the parties involved are aware of each other's identity. Some platforms, such as PeerJ, encourage open peer review, but it is not a requirement. Usually, traditional peer review occurs before the research is published, for various reasons, the first being as a filter to ensure that the paper is right for the publication, that it is a rigorous piece of research and that it provides new evidence on that particular topic. Once the paper has been published the peer review usually ceases.

Research may also be presented as a talk or a poster at a conference or delivered at a seminar in a university setting where an informal peer review can sometimes take place. Research may be commented on in discussion forums and on social media, written about in blogs and even covered in the media. All of this has the potential to be beneficial to the research's impact and measurable via tools like Altmetric.com, but it does not maximize the potential of an open research web. Open peer review platforms, whether pre or post publication, have the potential to stretch the conversation beyond that of traditional peer review, conference posters and presentations. Open peer review comes with a few caveats to ensure that its potential is maximized, and this is where problems can arise.

The benefits and problems of open peer review

Open peer review has many potential benefits for the scholarly communications within a research field or for individual researchers holding those conversations. Firstly, it can improve the quality of reviews because reviewers have to put their names to their comments. Traditional blind peer review and anonymous commenting provides some level of security for reviewers to say what they want, but this is not to say that they use blind peer review as a way to grind their axe. Nevertheless, reviewers are the gatekeepers and decide whether and how quickly a paper is published. There are examples of reviewers holding back research because it contains competing work, or because they wish to plagiarize it for their own publications and profile. There are also some extreme cases where reviewers have been hoodwinked by fictitious research, sometimes by researchers trying to test the peer review system, or by others out for ill-gotten gains. One high-profile case concerned 43 papers that were retracted by BioMed Central in 2015 when it became suspicious and began its own investigation into 50 published papers. In some cases authors have been found to be reviewing their own papers, and one high-profile case led to the retraction of 28 journal papers. The website Retraction Watch puts the total number of papers retracted on the grounds of being fake at about 170, but the true number is likely to be higher than that because fake papers could very well still exist in print.

Traditional peer review can be a frustrating process, given that the author generally does not know the identity of the reviewers and that it is very hard to discover who they are. In cases where there may be some wrongdoing in the review it can be hard to voice concerns about potential bias or malpractice, especially if the lead author is a junior academic. Opening up peer review has similar potential to altmetrics. Both are about a new openness in academia, as are other developments such as MOOCs, big data and open access. Pre-publication open peer review also provides an opportunity for the research community to identify inaccuracies before they are formally published. It is not uncommon for researchers to publish their findings, only to discover similar research with similar or quite different outcomes. Scientific research publication is restricted by the limitations of the publication model and, invariably, publications are still wholly textual, complete with tables, graphs, charts and images. They are not accompanied by sound and video, and pre-publication peer review comments are rarely accessible. The whole publishing process, like the research process, happens behind closed doors. Pre-publication peer review could open up research to a wider audience of experts who could offer their own insights and identify flaws that peer reviewers have missed. The old saying that too many cooks spoil the broth may carry some truth, but some research could benefit from open peer review, provided that the right checks and balances were in place, which would include permitting only authorized experts and authors to comment. Databases such as PubMed and its post-publication peer review platform PubMed Commons lay down strict criteria on who can comment. For PubMed, commenting is limited to authors of publications indexed in PubMed or those whom an author has invited to comment.

Altmetrics and open peer review have similar agendas, driven by those who are unhappy with the status quo. Both are about opening up research and making it more transparent for the benefit of researchers, funders and, to some extent, the general public. However, they do not share entirely the same support base, some authors favouring the one over the other. While many would like both to exist as part of a modern research environment, some see open peer review, primarily in the pre-publication format, as the true way to improve and measure research. Its value lies in the fact that it is not tied to numbers and charts, as is the case with citations and impact scores, but that it relies on objective, critical, expert opinion.

The history of open peer review

Open peer review is nothing new, and there were notable trials in the late 1990s by Smith (1999) and Godlee, Gale and Martyn (1998) in the leading medical journals *British Medical Journal (BMJ)* and *Journal of the American Medical Association*. In addition, the *BMJ* and other research publications accept letters, e-mail communications and Rapid Responses about research published in their journals. Despite some of the element of slowness or delay in these methods, they are a form of open post-publication peer review. There are also plenty of blogs and social media sites where researchers discuss others' work with an open attitude, and websites such as The Conversation enable academics to publish their ideas, thoughts and research to wider audiences. All of these audiences, including readers with no formal expertise in the area they are discussing, can then comment on the work directly. It would not take much time for any researcher to find some mention of their work on the web that goes beyond the usual citation.

Ford (2013) conducted a literature review of open peer review and discovered that there was no established definition of the term accepted by the scholarly research and publishing community. Instead, Ford (2013) identified several common characteristics of open peer review that describe the openness of the review process: signed review, disclosed review, editor-mediated review, transparent review and crowdsourced review. There are three further characteristics that describe review timing, similar to traditional peer review: pre-publication review, synchronous review and post-publication review.

The world is changing

Social media testifies to how individuals and groups have exploited a new openness on the web, yet in academia this has been less forthcoming. The model of academic peer review, in all its variants, pre-dates the first scholarly journal. Fitzpatrick (2011) notes its origins in the formation of the national academies in the 17th century. Not a lot has changed in peer review since then. The reasons are various, but are rooted in an academic culture that is still firmly rooted in the lecture-style presentation as the dominant teaching method, despite the existence of technologies and pedagogies to do otherwise. Nevertheless, there are genuine concerns about an open model of peer review. These range from fear of reviewer backlash to clashes of personality and reviewers feeling scrutinized by fellow reviewers. There is also the issue that some reviewers who are junior to the author they are reviewing may fear that their own career prospects could be affected. The issues are complicated and not based solely on ethical and practical reasons, but also on legal ones. Yet, with other changes afoot in academia that are referred to in this book, most notably MOOCs, open access, impact, altmetrics and big data, it seems that the noise around open peer review will just get louder. To some extent open peer review is a very subjective issue, as it is not just about academic rigour but also about identity, and not just the identity of the reviewers and authors, but also that of research as a whole. As with social media and altmetrics, it is an opportunity for research to open itself up, warts and all. In an ideal world, research would benefit from absolute openness on a global scale, but there is some research that cannot be discussed, or that concerns sensitive topics that could spark fierce debate. Take any research relating to religion, politics or sexuality, all very emotive topics. Some academics would find it hard to retain balance and focus in post-publication peer review, open or otherwise. These issues and many others will no doubt be covered more comprehensively as more platforms and websites explore open peer review. The remainder of this chapter investigates the leading academic open peer review platforms and how they operate, looking at the different approaches taken by ten of the platforms.

Traditional blind peer review

Alongside open peer review, several models of peer review are currently practised, the standard models being single and double blind. Single-blind review is where the author's identity is usually revealed to reviewers and double-blind review is where all identities are kept hidden. As Smith (2006) highlights, people have a great many fantasies about peer review, one of the most powerful being that it is a highly objective, reliable and consistent process; yet the fact is that many are discontented with the model of traditional blind peer review and view it only in negative terms as lacking in rewards, slow in return, inconsistent and occasionally open to fraud and bad behaviour. Despite its key, idealized role in the history of scholarship, peer review has at times been subject to criticism (Sullivan, 2014), while the traditional academic publishing model has been criticized for being somewhat behind the rest of the modern publishing industry. Given modern-day communications and publishing technologies, a large part of this criticism is fair, when we consider that a piece of research can take over a year to complete, and then just as long to get published. After such a length of time, work in that research area could have moved on, with new methods, technologies and ideas all appearing. Open peer review has the potential to reduce this inertia, while also making researchers aware of potential future collaborators or similar research already being undertaken.

A review of the platforms

Whether we like it or not, technology is ingrained into how we work in research and support. Technology on the internet should never drive *how* we work, but invariably it has a very large impact. Often, technologies, whether web or otherwise, are created when someone sees a problem that needs to be solved or that there is a gap in the market. Often, technologists try to scan the horizon and guess where a solution might be needed for a future problem. In academia there are many problems, some of which can be referred to as 'wicked problems' (Churchman, 1967). Peer review could be considered a wicked problem, one that is difficult or impossible to resolve because of a variety of factors (which are often difficult to recognize) such as its incompleteness, contradiction and changing requirements. Open peer review via discussion forums, post-publication comment and social media has been heralded by some as the solution to that problem. As you will read below, the possible solutions are perhaps just the start of a revolution that may produce many different options and a growing number of new platforms to help facilitate open peer review. At present there is only a small collection of established and fledgling platforms, some of which are seeking to make their own imprint on the scholarly communication landscape. Often the narrow focus of niche technologies is due to limited resources, and the notion that it is much better to do a few things right rather than many things averagely. The web is very good at homogenizing society, and once a platform or technology starts to create attention the critical mass soon follows. As more academics embrace online tools for scholarly communication, more are likely to follow in order to see what all the fuss is about. In a natural progression, the increase in attention and usage will lead to an increase in the number of platforms. The list of platforms reviewed below is by no means exhaustive but it does account for much of the current activity and discussion around open peer review.

F1000Research

Faculty of 1000 combines three different strands, all committed to publishing research and communicating its findings. First there is F1000Prime, which is a personalized recommendation system for biomedical research articles from F1000. Like *PLOS ONE*, F1000Research is an open science journal that tries to speed up publishing turnaround times with a transparent referee model. The second strand is F1000Posters, which previously had an independent existence as a platform for academics to host their own posters. The third strand is the most recent addition, F1000Workspace, which allows scientists to collect, write and discuss scientific literature.

F1000Research's approach to peer review is to be totally open, publishing referees' comments and subsequent replies by the authors.

As in the traditional blind peer review process, submissions are 'approved' at once, or 'approved with reservations', or 'not approved'. The thinking applied by F1000Research is that this ensures that not only is the author's research revealed to the wider world, but so also are the abilities and comments of the reviewer. The whole commenting process is date stamped and, unlike most peer review, gives a right of reply to the author. Visitors to F1000Research can track the conversation and even discuss the article at the foot of the publication page. They can also see a timeline of the research publishing process. Referees' reports can be cited in F1000Research and published under a Creative Commons By Attribution License. A DOI (digital object identifier) is assigned to every referee report, thus allowing it to be cited independently from the article.

Open Review

Open Review is part of the ResearchGate platform and enables researchers to publish open and transparent reviews of any papers they have read, worked with or cited. ResearchGate evaluates research from a different angle and asks if it is reproducible. Registered users choose an article that is listed on ResearchGate and can then go through a simple review process that involves answering simple 'yes' and 'no' questions relating to the research's methodology, analyses, references, findings and conclusions. Supporting resources can be attached and the reviewer is invited to leave free-text statements related to each question. The completed review and scores given to each aspect can be viewed, and over time becomes collated with any further reviews. Reviewers can add the names of other colleagues involved in the review process, but only with their consent.

PeerJ

PeerJ is an open access peer-reviewed scientific journal with a focus on publishing research in the biological and medical sciences. PeerJ employs a points system for authors and commentators as an incentive to publish and comment on research. This incentive acts much like many typical massive online multiplayer games, where achievements and positive actions are rewarded with points. The more you interact, the more you are rewarded. A reviewer can gain anything from 100 points for being an editor or an author on a PeerJ article to just one point for receiving an 'up vote' for a reply to a question or comment. The system is not without its flaws, as critics of altmetrics would agree, based on the issue of attention over quality of content. Gaining a lot of points may not necessarily mean that you are providing quality to the system. As in the multiplayer game analogy, some players may be at the top of the rankings purely because they can put in the excessive hours to play, rather than because they are the most skillful players. Nevertheless, PeerJ is an interesting take on the open peer review model, and one that could appeal to the more competitive among academics.

PeerJ hosts tables showing the top authors and reviewers, which can be filtered by topic area and publication date and show who have asked the most questions and given the most answers. The question-and-answer approach is very different from the commenting seen on other platforms and presents another option for opening up dialogue between authors and commentators. At present, as for other similar platforms, there is not a lot of commenting activity. The points ranking system will appeal to some researchers, especially those with a competitive streak, although, on the flipside, it may make others feel equally uncomfortable. As with altmetrics, some academics like to see their research measured in tweets and downloads as well as by traditional metrics, so the points system will appeal to them. PeerJ's points system is a clear attempt to encourage academics to engage more with scholarly communications, especially via this platform. But, as with open peer review as a whole, the approach is certain to divide the academic community.

Peerage of Science

The website Peerage of Science is not explicitly an open peer review platform but it does give authors who submit content the option of providing their details to reviewers. Peerage of Science aims to provide the opportunity for authors to have their manuscripts reviewed by qualified, non-affiliated peers. While it encourages authors to remain anonymous, this is not compulsory. It would be interesting to see who would be willing to reveal their name at such an early stage of review. There are some merits in authors' submitting their manuscripts to such a model, while it could also have the same problems as traditional peer review. For researchers, especially early-career ones who do not have contact with peers in their field, it is worth investigating. But any kind of early review platform could also become a hub for predatory journals and academics, the latter taking the opportunity to steal emerging ideas and manuscripts. On the other side of the coin, however, there is the opportunity for academics to build their reputations and skills as reviewers of research. Peerage of Science operates like an agency that matches reviewers with manuscripts. The problem with such a model is that reviewers could build their reputations on the basis of quantity of reviews, not quality. However, given the difficulty that some authors have in sourcing early appropriate opinions on their work, the benefits could outweigh the risks.

PLOS ONE

PLOS ONE was launched by the Public Library of Science (PLOS), an open access, mostly traditional, peer-reviewed scientific journal publisher. Pre-publication article submissions are usually blind reviewed, although reviewers have the option to go down the open route. The pure open peer review happens after the paper has been published. Reviews and comments can be submitted by registered *PLOS ONE* members only. *PLOS ONE* has the advantage of being the world's largest journal, based on the number of papers it publishes. It has a mandate to make research more discoverable and engaging, while speeding up the publication process. When a registered user leaves a comment it is with the desired purpose of adding to the research or clarifying aspects of it. This involves identifying and linking to materials and evidence that will form threaded discussions on the published research. *PLOS ONE* sets no limits to the length of a commenter's post – it can be as simple or as detailed as they wish. The commenter can focus on a single part of the research, for example the results, the methodology or the conclusion, and is under no obligation to write more than just a few lines. Some commenters may decide to provide more in-depth reviews about the paper as a whole. Commenting on papers in *PLOS ONE* is open only to registered users, who must identify any competing interests. *PLOS ONE* has a clear set of rules for commenters, which states that commenters must not post:

1 remarks that could be interpreted as allegations of misconduct
2 unsupported assertions or statements
3 inflammatory or insulting language.

Anyone who breaches these rules will be removed from *PLOS ONE* and their account will be disabled. This will not prevent the more mischievous of commentators from creating a new account, but we have to remember that this and other kinds of abuse are a problem that is not exclusive to open peer review websites.

PubMed Commons

Anyone working in life sciences and biomedical research and support will be aware of PubMed, a huge, publicly accessible search engine that accesses the Medline database of references and abstracts in the life sciences and biomedical research field. PubMed launched Commons as a platform for the authors of papers hosted in PubMed to post comments on research in the Medline database. Only researchers who are authors of PubMed-hosted content are eligible to comment, and this creates a barrier that prevents just anyone leaving inaccurate, unevidenced or mischievous comments. The e-mail addresses of eligible authors are collected from the National Institutes of Health, the Wellcome Trust and authors' e-mail addresses held in PubMed and PubMed Central. Authors who are not listed in these databases can ask a colleague who is already registered on the system to send them an invitation to join. The open review is transparent because anyone posting comments must use their real name and disclose any conflicts of interest.

Publons

Publons (Figure 11.1) looks at open peer review from a different angle by focusing more on the reviewer. The primary aim of Publons is to highlight and assist researchers and their reviewing activity, rather than the publication side of academia. As already discussed, peer review is not generally regarded as one of the most enjoyable aspects of academia. To some extent it is regarded as a necessary evil; why review someone else's research when you could be creating your own? Because much of

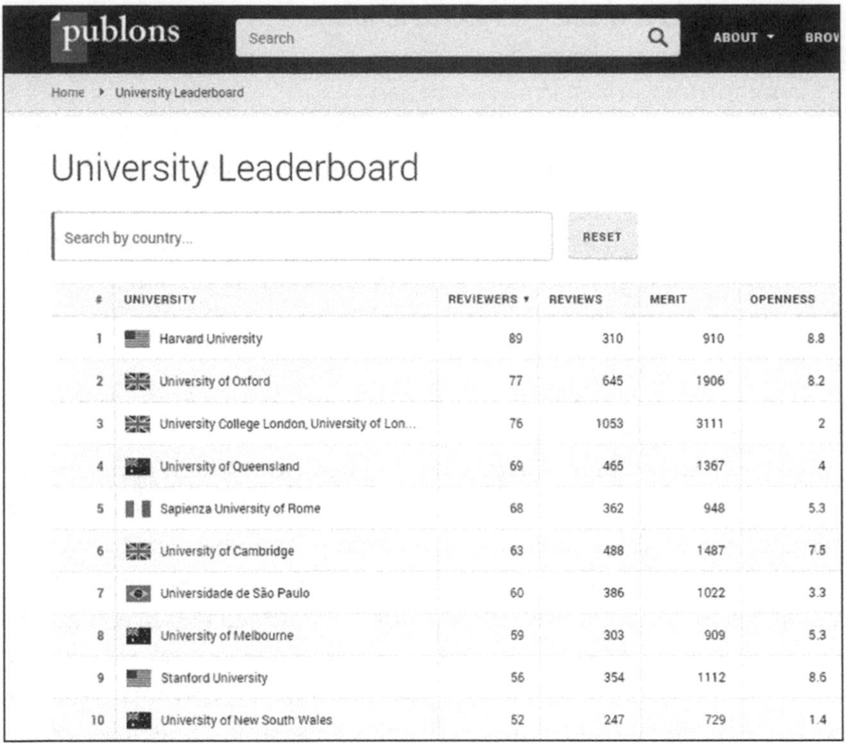

#	UNIVERSITY	REVIEWERS ▾	REVIEWS	MERIT	OPENNESS
1	Harvard University	89	310	910	8.8
2	University of Oxford	77	645	1906	8.2
3	University College London, University of Lon...	76	1053	3111	2
4	University of Queensland	69	465	1367	4
5	Sapienza University of Rome	68	362	948	5.3
6	University of Cambridge	63	488	1487	7.5
7	Universidade de São Paulo	60	386	1022	3.3
8	University of Melbourne	59	303	909	5.3
9	Stanford University	56	354	1112	8.6
10	University of New South Wales	52	247	729	1.4

Figure 11.1 *Publons*

it happens behind closed doors, it is not so often formally acknowledged as part of an academic's public profile. In an attempt to correct that, Publons was set up with the idea that academics should get credit for their peer-review work. Peer reviewing is an important part of an academic's career-building strategy. It can benefit a researcher's CV and promotion prospects, and there is the bonus of getting to see emerging research, but because of the existing anonymous culture it is not always so easy to measure, especially in comparison with the roles of editor or author. Publons' strategy is to work with reviewers, publishers, universities and funding agencies to turn peer review into a measurable research output. It does this by collecting peer-review information from reviewers and publishers and using the data to create reviewer profiles. Publishers then verify this information so that researchers can add it to their CVs. This allows reviewers to control how each review is displayed on their profile, whether that be blind, open or published. Reviewers can add pre-publication reviews that they write for journals as well as post-publication reviews.

PubPeer

PubPeer is an online journal club that allows users to search for papers via DOIs, PubMed Identifiers, arXiv IDs, keywords and authors, among other options. PubPeer's aim is to create a digital community of academics who engage in commentary on and discussion of published research results. Researchers can comment on almost any scientific article that is published with a DOI or any pre-print in arXiv. They can also browse a comprehensive list of journals and comments. At this time, however, as in so many other commenting platforms, the majority of titles only have one or two comments. Anonymous commenting is possible in PubPeer, although as a safeguard users are required to sign up. One problem with anonymous comments, especially when they are posted in large numbers, is when they are not moderated. PubPeer does moderate comments before publishing them, although how quickly an anonymous comment is accepted will depend on the number of items in the queue. Any kind of anonymous commenting is always susceptible to trolling and abuse, quite simply because those posting such comments feel they have an extra level of protection and distance from what they say. PubPeer gained extra attention in 2014 when a researcher filed a lawsuit over anonymous comments. The researcher claimed that the comments resulted in their losing a job offer, following accusations of misconduct in their research.

ScienceOpen

ScienceOpen is an open peer review platform with full transparency of reviewers and comments. The website is an independent publishing platform that makes its referee reports available under a Creative Commons By Attribution License. In essence, it is part publishing platform, part social network. As with some of the other platforms listed here, ScienceOpen enables reviewers to build a public collection of reviews. The purpose of this is to showcase researchers not just as authors but as critical reviewers. A user's registered account can be automatically synchronized with their Open Researcher and Contributor ID (ORCiD) profile.

The Winnower

The Winnower is one of the smaller platforms that is committed to open research. It was set up at around the same time as PeerJ, Publons and Peerage of Science, and attempts to extend the long tail of discovery and dialogue about research. Like some of the other platforms mentioned here, The Winnower has a mandate that 'is founded on the principle that all ideas should be openly discussed, debated and archived'. Like similar small, independent online research start-ups, The Winnower was the idea of a PhD student; and, like so many other things in academia, small, new platforms can be less attractive to academics. Academics have a need for evidence; why should they use a technology or website when no one else is using it? This also applies to using a new technology to critically review someone else's work, especially when they compare it with large, established entities such as *PLOS ONE* and PubMed. It is increasingly hard for web start-ups to break into an already crowded market unless they can improve on existing models. An interesting experiment and an alternative measurement by The Winnower are The Grain and The Chaff web pages (Figure 11.2). The 'grain' features publications with more than 1000 citations or an altmetric score above

Figure 11.2 *The Winnower's 'The Grain and The Chaff'*

250. At the other end, the 'chaff' features papers that were pulled from publication and gives a voice to rejected authors to write about their research, rather than just providing a simple a 'name and shame' list.

A wealth of options

The variety of available options for open peer review (Table 11.1) is indicative of some of the issues that not only open peer review platforms but academic technologies as a whole must address. To some extent there is a drive for learning and communication technologies to find and lead their own markets. This invariably means trying to find the right technology for yourself and the academics you work with. As we have seen, many research websites fall by the wayside, and that includes some of those mentioned in this book. Some run out of money, some out of energy, and others simply do not take off. The sad fact is that some of the technologies covered in this book will disappear, taking with them some great ideas and features. There are many facets to the delivery and management even of something so seemingly simple as open peer review. This is because of the diversity of opinions on how best to improve scholarly measurement and communication via peer review, whether that be open or blind. As shown by the platforms covered in this chapter, being open is not necessarily a two-way relationship, nor is it compulsory. There are those who believe that open peer review can work only if every aspect of it is transparent, while others prefer some degree of anonymity, and yet others still wish to remain in the shadows of blind peer review. The ten platforms covered in this chapter are just part of the first wave of open peer review platforms. Others are sure to follow and we will no doubt see further iterations of open peer review.

The platforms covered in this chapter all have similar themes, but they take different approaches to open peer review. Some focus on commenting, others are more discussion based, and yet others employ a points systems, in addition to questions and answers. There are alternative metrics, such as The Winnower's 'Wheat and Chaff', and systems that offer reward and formal acknowledgement to those who spend time reviewing others' content. Some options in open peer review are more popular than others, depending on each researcher's set of professional beliefs. Some researchers congregate around platforms that

Table 11.1 Pre- and post-publication open review and comment platforms

Platform	Open pre- or post-publication review/comment	Level of openness	Owner	Year established	Key audience	Other services	Creative Commons license
F1000Research	Post	Open	Faculty of 1000	2002 as Faculty of Biology (now F1000 Prime)	Life sciences	F1000Prime F1000Posters F1000Specialists F1000Journal Clubs	NA
Open Review	Post	Open	ResearchGate	2008 as ResearchGate, 2014 as Open Review	Non-specific	ResearchGate	NA
Peerage of Science	Pre	Open – Onymous (Peerage of Science, https://www.peerageofscience.org/onymous-peer-review/) (Peerage of Science, https://www.peerageofscience.org/onymous-peer-review/)	Janne Kotiaho, Mikko Mökkönen, Janne-Tuomas Seppänen	2012	Science		NA
PeerJ	Pre and post	Open review encouraged	Jason Hoyt, Pete Binfield	2012	Biology, medicine	PeerJ Computer Science PeerJ PrePrints	CC BY 4.0
PLOS ONE	Pre and post	Optional for pre-publication; Open for post-publication comment	Public Library of Science	2006	Medicine, science		CC BY 4.0
Publons	Pre and post	Optional	Andrew Preston, Daniel Johnston	2012	Non-specific		CC BY 4.0
PubMed Commons	Post	Open	US National Library of Medicine	2015	Biomedicine	PubMed	CC BY 3.0
PubPeer	Post	Optional	NA	2013	Non-specific		NA
ScienceOpen	Pre and post	Open	ScienceOpen	2013	Non-specific	ScienceOpen Research ScienceOpen Posters	CC BY 4.0
The Winnower	Pre and post	Open	Josh Nicholson	2012	Non-specific		CC BY 4.0

focus on their specific research areas; and, as in any area of the web that allows for comment and discussion, some academics will feel that they have nothing to hide, and embrace open peer review to discuss research openly. At the other end of the spectrum are academics who are fearful of what they may read about their own hard work and are reluctant to interact with negative comments, constructive or otherwise. Deciding which is the best, most active and rewarding platform is no doubt a matter of concern and confusion for some researchers and reviewers. We also have to heed other potential problems that are not exclusive to peer review, such as the problem of predatory journals and conferences, as it is likely that we could see similar problems in open peer review. Only time will tell.

Other notable mentions

This chapter has looked at some of the more prominent and established open peer review platforms, but is worth also mentioning some other platforms.

PaperCritic was created by the Mendeley API and works with Mendeley to monitor papers in your reference collection and via your Mendeley contacts list. It ceased posting updates on its various social media platforms in early 2014, which is never a good sign for a tool that is based on social interaction.

Another interesting tool was Chapter Swap, which focused on the grassroots of research by providing an opportunity for authors to swap draft copies of their work for review. Chapter Swap aimed at the postgraduate and postdoctoral market and those working in the arts and humanities. Like PaperCritic, its once-active Twitter feed ceased in 2013, indicating that the service was no longer active.

Libre is an open peer review platform that is hosted by Open Scholar C.I.C. and operates solely within the academic community. Its aim is to switch roles and put authors in the driving seat of the review process. It does this with transparency and openness, publishing content under a Creative Commons license. At the time of writing this chapter, Libre was still in a testing phase but potential users were being encouraged to sign up in time for the first stable release.

Science Open Review (not to be confused with Science Open or

SciOR) is based at Queens University, Canada, and connects authors with reviewers in author-led non-blind peer review.

The *Journal of Visualized Experiments* (*JOVE*) is a platform that has been gaining much traction since its first appearance in 2006. It is the leading online video journal and has a remit to support the replication of published research. Its pre-publication review model is anonymous, as is part of the post-publication comment. *JOVE* is included here on the basis that it allows users to leave comments that include their first name and the initial of their surname, which in some cases may be enough to allow recognition.

A mixed-model approach

Research is driven by the idea of solving problems, improving systems, creating a better understanding and bringing about enlightenment. Open peer review, like altmetrics, sets out to do the same for the research process and how we communicate scholarly work. If we think of the old and the new – citations, blind review, indexes and impact scores alongside altmetrics, Snowball Metrics and open peer review – as steps towards a better understanding of research, we should be able to move to a better place than we currently occupy. The alternative is for LIS professionals and their research colleagues to become bogged down in a mire of processes and technologies, all competing, all offering a confusing multitude of choice. That said, as we have seen, there is invention resulting from the advancement of scholarly communication. One novel idea that has been suggested is to give a digital badge those who have actively contributed to a piece of research. This badge would reflect their role in that particular piece of research. Cantor and Gero (2015) propose the creation of an R-index scale of reviewer recognition. We have to consider the connection with and purpose of open access – to remove access barriers, not quality filters (Suber, 2012). We have yet to see the true impact of open access, despite its increasing adoption and the fact that academics have been pushing for this model since as early as the 1950s. Although the connection between open access and open peer review is obvious to some, it is less so to others. Ford (2013) argued that while open access and open peer review go hand in hand, open peer review does not need to happen only in open access journals.

Conclusion

Most of the open peer review platforms currently have just a few comments on some research articles; the majority of articles have none. This is understandable, considering factors such as lack of awareness, permission, confidence and the all-important critical mass. Why start a conversation in a room where there is no one else to listen? In time, this could change. For now, despite the huge amount of published research, navigating and responding to posted comments is quite manageable. However, as we have seen with platforms such as Twitter and Facebook, once a connection joins a social network, others will follow. We may reach a stage where some channels become so popular as they open up scholarly communication that we find ourselves dealing with a cacophony of noise if the discussion is not properly moderated. Perhaps we should look to the words of Shirky (2008), who argues that our problem is one not of information overload but of filter failure. We have to consider whether encouraging researchers to comment more than they have done up to now would be productive or disruptive. Tasks such as responding to and leaving comments could be another disruptive interruption to researchers' focus, especially if a topic became increasingly debated, argued or even heated. The disruptive aspect of social media and discussion forums is very noticeable in the non-academic environment. The temptation to continually look to see if anyone has responded to your latest update or message can be overpowering. As in any kind of debate or argument, the temptation to have the last word can be strong. Yet open peer review, in particular the post-publication type, needs human interaction in the form of researchers' comments (preferably constructive ones) if it is to blossom and to benefit research. The web has broken down many of the high walls and silos within which researchers work, but there is more to be done. Many researchers still operate within a system in which their work does not appear above the parapet until it is published or delivered in a conference talk. They miss opportunities not only to share and discuss work early but also to be aware of similar research taking place elsewhere. Of course not all research can be open, and no open peer review initiative can discuss certain sensitive or strategic information that has to stay out of sight. For the research that is not shrouded in secrecy, researchers already have the tools covered in this chapter, as well as the many others such as Twitter or Mendeley. Using these technologies they can get a feel for what relevant research is going on around them. Open review of and commenting on published research can help to identify incorrect findings. The potential benefits of a new openness are succinctly highlighted by David Goldstein, Director of Duke University Centre for Human Genome Variation. Goldstein says: 'When some of these things sit around in scientific literature for a long time, they can do damage: they can influence what people work on, they can influence whole fields' (Mandavilli 2011).

Peer review as we know it may not be perfect but, as LIS professionals and researchers learn to understand the social web in its many forms, it could become better. The social web has the potential to become more useful both as a formal and an informal platform for discussion and knowledge sharing within the academic community. Given that we have the tools and that many are now firmly established, it makes sense to explore every possible option. Blind and open peer review currently co-exist and there is no reason for that not to continue. The case for both open and blind peer review is no different from that for altmetrics, which has often been regarded by its detractors as a completely new alternative to traditional measurement by citations. Proponents of altmetrics are now promoting the idea of alternative indicators, rather than whole measurement. Open peer review platforms need to be clear in their aims and to explain those clearly to researchers, commentators and reviewers alike. As with social media, it is doubtful that we will see every researcher using these platforms, and even if they become standardized, formalized and part of the research cycle, there is still likely to be resistance in some quarters. Many academics are likely to feel vulnerable in making their research open for comment, yet the reality is that this happens already, often without their knowing about it. Research that makes it into the public domain, especially via media coverage, is exposed to open review, and not always by peers but by the sometimes highly critical, often inexperienced, general public. Open peer review is nothing new and has been discussed, theorized and trialled for some time, but remains the junior partner of the traditional model of peer review. The existing open peer review platforms still have some way to go before they attract a critical mass.

All the while, it is increasingly important, if open peer review is to be a worthwhile exercise for reviewers and authors, that it be structured, and supported by moderation and authentication. If not, as Van Noorden (2014) asks, 'will online comments look more like a scattered hodgepodge of reviews, comments and discussions across websites unlinked to original publications?' Whatever happens, it is likely that, regardless of formal or informal peer review, someone could still comment on social media on your or a fellow researcher's work. Whether or not you respond remains your choice.

References

Cantor, M. and Gero, S. (2015) The Missing Metric: quantifying contributions of reviewers, *Royal Society Open Science*, **2** (2), http://rsos. royalsocietypublishing.org/content/royopensci/2/2/140540.full.pdf.

Churchman, C. W. (1967) Wicked Problems, *Management Science*, **14** (4), B-141–2.

Fitzpatrick, K. (2011) *Planned Obsolescence: publishing, technology, and the future of the academy*, New York University Press

Ford, E. (2013) Defining and Characterizing Open Peer Review: a review of the literature, *Journal of Scholarly Publishing*, **44** (4), 311–26, http://muse.jhu. edu/journals/journal_of_scholarly_publishing/v044/44.4.ford.html.

Godlee, F., Gale, C. and Martyn, C. (1998) Effect on the Quality of Peer Review of Blinding Reviewers and Asking Them to Sign Their Reports: a randomized controlled trial, *JAMA*, **280** (3), 237–40, http://jama. jamanetwork.com/article.aspx?articleid=187748.

Mandavilli, A. (2011) Trial by Twitter, *Nature*, www.axeleratio.com/news/trial_by_twitter_nature2011.pdf.

Shirky, C. (2008) It's Not Information Overload. It's filter failure. In *Web 2.0 Expo*, Web 2.0 Expo, www.web2expo.com/webexny2008/public/schedule/detail/4817.

Smith, R. (1999) Opening Up BMJ Peer Review: a beginning that should lead to complete transparency, *British Medical Journal*, **318** (January), 4–5.

Smith, R. (2006) Peer Review: a flawed process at the heart of science and journals, *Journal of the Royal Society of Medicine*, **99** (4), 178–82, http://jrs.sagepub.com/content/99/4/178.short.

Suber, P. (2012) *Open Access First*, MIT Press.

Sullivan, M. (2014) *Peer Review and Open Access*, OpenStax.

Van Noorden, R. (2014) *The New Dilemma of Online Peer Review: too many places to post?*, Nature Newsblog, http://blogs.nature.com/news/2014/03/the-new-dilemma-of-online-peer-review-too-many-places-to-post.html.

Useful link

http://retractionwatch.com/.

Recommended reading

Much has already been written on the subject of open peer review, pre and post publication. Two of the more notable web articles and one report are listed below.

Anderson, K. (2014) Stick to Your Ribs: the problems with calling comments 'post-publication peer-review', http://scholarlykitchen.sspnet.org/2014/04/15/stick-to-your-ribs-the-problems-with-calling-comments-post-publication-peer-review/.

House of Commons Science and Technology Committee (2011) *Eighth Report – peer review in scientific publications*, www.publications.parliament.uk/pa/cm201012/cmselect/cmsctech/856/85602.htm.

Zwaan, R. (2014) Pre-publication posting and post-publication review will facilitate the correction of errors and will ultimately strengthen published submissions, http://blogs.lse.ac.uk/impactofsocialsciences/2013/04/19/pre-publication-posting-and-post-publication-review/.

CHAPTER 12

Conclusion

Andy Tattersall

Introduction

This final chapter considers the evidence from the preceding chapters and attempts to summarize where the future lies for altmetrics and associated developments. As with the rest of the book, this chapter aims to give readers a realistic view of developments and of the benefits and pitfalls that LIS professionals face when contemplating new ways of incorporating technology into their work processes. The chapter aims to provide a picture of the here and now and looks to a future that holds many possibilities, but also uncertainties.

Altmetrics: a work in progress

Like so much published research that is supported by LIS professionals, the ideas and changes captured in this book are a work in progress. By the time this book is published altmetrics will be just over five years old. In relation to the creation of the web that is about one-fifth of its history. The web has existed for about one generation but has changed the lives of many demographic groups, academics being one of them. No one could have predicted what the web would look like five years ago and it is virtually impossible to say what it will look like in the future. However, what we can say about the current state of web and social technology adoption in relation to research publishing and communication is that it is in its greatest ever state of flux and change. The evidence presented in this book and other similar titles is that the academic community has been slow to adapt to the opportunities brought about by the internet. Universities and research centres were quick to make themselves visible on the web in the early 1990s, but beyond that there has been inertia, or certainly confusion over which areas to focus on. Other industries, including the arts, media and especially pornography, have seen the value in spreading their content across the web in easily accessible formats. But academic content is no less important or interesting to online communities. The biggest problem in terms of the slow uptake is two-fold. First is the confusion over which technologies and platforms to use, in addition to the creation of learning initiatives; second are the cultural issues surrounding change and the adoption of new ways of communicating and measuring research, which take many academics away from their comfort zone.

Much of the change and technology adoption that we are seeing in academia – altmetrics, open peer review and big data – is being championed by PhD students or early career researchers. Many of these champions who started platforms such as Mendeley, Altmetric.com, figshare and Impactstory saw that academia was stagnating in a technology-led economy. The old methods of scholarly publishing, measurement, sharing and communication are no longer fit for purpose and we are in the midst of a rapid and exciting period of change. This change will have winners and losers. On the one hand, some of the old dinosaurs of academic publishing may become extinct during our working lives; on the other hand, we will also see many small academic web start-ups burn brightly for short periods before falling by the wayside. How we communicate and measure research by the end of the decade and the next Research Excellent Framework (REF) in 2020 may be very different from how we did it at the start of the decade.

What we can say about the web is that it will continue to change and to diverge into specialist areas. Technology will continue to embed itself within academia, regardless of any resistance. The web is the greatest agent of change within academia, but it still needs the people and the reason for that change to be positive. It is a case not of whether but of when we will see a paradigm shift as the research community embraces new web technologies on a large scale. Digital advocates such as

Baroness Martha Lane Fox, who co-founded Lastminute.com, believe that the future functioning society will be underpinned by a wholesale uptake of web – but it might not just happen just yet. As more digital-native students forge careers for themselves in academia, in time research, its communication and its measurement will become one ecosystem with many arteries underpinned by technology and the web. LIS professionals have always adapted to change in one way or another and they are conversant in knowledge and information systems that wax and wane with the times. Altmetrics is one such system. With it come a wealth of challenges and, more importantly, opportunities. It comes down to a question of whether LIS professionals want to take advantage of them.

Opportunities if you take them

Academics carrying out their work, whether in an office, a lab or out in the field, are now totally reliant on the web for large parts of the research cycle. If we imagine that we removed all of the road network, then travel would continue but at a much slower, fractured pace. The web has become the road network of the research process. If academics were given restricted use of the web their work would be negatively impacted upon. Yet many academics are imposing limitations on themselves in terms of how they engage with the web in the course of their research processes. As this book has identified, many are not aware of what tools are available to aid scholarly communication and research measurement. This is where the LIS professional has a part to play and, more notably, an opportunity to seize. Naturally, there will be no call to arms, and, given that LIS professionals are often stretched capacity-wise, massive change is unrealistic. However, many LIS professionals are involved in initiatives that are closely allied to altmetrics. Altmetric.com spotted that connection and has created tools specifically for librarians. Also, many LIS professionals have the right sets of skills to engage with the academic community. They are often embedded in the academic community as knowledge and support experts and many are skilled trainers and communicators and treat their roles as a vocation, aiming to support their colleagues in every way possible. Altmetrics, along with MOOCs, big data, open access and peer review, presents opportunities, and exciting ones at that. LIS professionals too must see it as an opportunity, rather than as a barrier, a problem and just more stuff to manage. Naturally, engaging with any new way of working brings problems, learning curves, being out of your comfort zone and additional workload. For those who are willing and able new ways of working can provide an extra skill to an already diverse set of talents within the LIS community. While many have already engaged with altmetrics and it is not a new thing for them, for the majority of the academic community it is still very early days. The opportunities are two-fold. First, when LIS professionals develop their own technical and communication skills, they make themselves more valuable to their institution. Second, they are able to help a huge, knowledge-based workforce to adapt to the changes happening within academia. It is important to remember that just because academics may not engage in social networks, media and altmetrics they are not necessarily unwilling. They may simply not realize that there is support to learn about them. The amount of support available from LIS professionals is finite, whereas the demand for it from academics and research students can at times feel infinite. Some of the tools and ideas covered in this book may go some way towards stretching the finite resources further. As for any modern instructional support, the best solutions are those that reduce duplication and repetition. Instructional videos, blogs and documents in VLEs could be as useful to academics as they are to students if they are used correctly. While face-to-face tuition will always be an effective and core instructional process, it is important for liaison and specialist LIS professionals to be aware of the limits of their resources.

Change is afoot

There is no doubt that a great change is happening in academia, and technology is enabling it to happen. MOOCs, open access, open peer review, big data and altmetrics all have great potential and are underpinned by the web and associated technologies. That word 'impact' will continue to reverberate across academia, and how we value and measure research and its impact will become increasingly important. For researchers and universities pushing their content and messages into the ether, there needs to be some kind of feedback loop. Altmetrics has a big part to play here and is already being taken up by many institutions, funding bodies and individuals.

It is important to remember that the technology should never drive the change. Just as there must be a pedagogy to apply learning technology to, so also there need to be clear reasons why researchers should embrace new ways of working, using technology and the web. These reasons need to be clearly set out, and built where possible on evidence. But much innovation comes about from a 'gut feeling' or by following trends. Therein lies the rub, that for new technologies and new ways of working there is sometimes little or no evidence, just 'gut feeling' or a sense of adventure. At some point researchers will have to consider engaging with some of the technologies that Web 2.0 has brought us. Those might be academic social networks, cloud-based reference management, Twitter, blogs or even altmetrics. Failure to engage could leave individuals, institutions, even nations drastically lagging behind their peers and competitors. Setting up a Mendeley, figshare or Piirus profile is a start, but it will be of little use if the user fails to upload content or connect with peers. There is much truth in the saying that you get out only what you put in.

Conclusion

Despite the rapid changes taking place in academia, of which altmetrics is a part, we have to be realistic about what we can achieve for now. But we should also be open to the multitude of possibilities that technology can provide. It is easy to pick holes in the existing publishing model, citations, the impact factor, h index and peer review. This is a system that is entrenched in the research community, but it is one that could change beyond recognition, should academia be brave enough to take the leap. However, most proponents of altmetrics and open peer review have never favoured wholesale change, and to some extent research is caught between a rock and a hard place. By first accepting that the current methods of measurement, communication and sharing are deeply flawed we can start to look where to improve on them. That, however, is not going to happen overnight, or in the next year, or even in the next decade, as it is too big a problem to solve quickly, with too many competing agendas.

Altmetrics should be considered as alternative an indicator, and open peer review as a valuable way of communicating and assessing research quality. With the right checks and balances in place, better use of these innovations can improve scholarly communication and collaboration. Like two tectonic plates coming together, it would be conceivable to think that the old and the new can come together to create a new academic landscape. It is very likely that by 2020 we will see a very different web, and a myriad of new research technologies built on it. How academics and LIS professionals chart that new landscape we can only wait to see.

Key points

- Altmetrics is not a replacement for traditional metrics such as impact factor and citation counts.
- Where possible, altmetrics should be considered as an alternative indicator of scholarly communications and reach.
- Altmetrics is not necessarily an indicator of research quality.
- The development of altmetrics and scholarly communications will continue to evolve; it is likely we are at the very beginning of the era of digital academia.
- Those who are engaging with the web and altmetrics as part of their research workflow are more likely to reap the benefit in terms of successful impact and discovering where their research is being shared, discussed and repurposed.
- Employing altmetric and scholarly communication tools can make LIS professionals and researchers more technology savvy and, in the long run, potentially more valuable to digitally driven institutions.
- There is still much confusion about the growing number of academic web platforms and which ones are the best for academics to use. LIS professionals can help academics to navigate their way through the myriad of tools available to them.
- LIS professionals have much to gain by embracing altmetrics and other scholarly communication tools and becoming expert in how best to use these tools.

Web resources

Altmetrics, a Manifesto: http://altmetrics.org/manifesto/.

Altmetric.com Blog: www.altmetric.com/blog/.

Altmetrics Conference: www.altmetricsconference.com/.

Altmetrics – What they are and why they should matter to the library and information community: www.cilip.org.uk/blog/altmetrics-what-they-are-why-they-should-matter-library-information-community.

Digital Science's Blogs: https://www.digital-science.com/blog/.

HEFCE Review of Metrics in research assessment: www.hefce.ac.uk/rsrch/metrics/.

Impactstory Blog: http://blog.impactstory.org/.

Jobs.ac.uk Digital Academic Blog: https://blogs.jobs.ac.uk/the-digital-academic/.

LSE Impact Blog: http://blogs.lse.ac.uk/impactofsocialsciences/.

Further reading

Bastow, S., Dunleavy, P. and Tinkler, J. (2014) *The Impact of the Social Sciences: how academics and their research make a difference*, Sage Publications Ltd.

Daly, I. and Brophy Haney, A. (eds) (2014) *53 Interesting Ways to Communicate Your Research*, The Professional and Higher Partnership Ltd.

Denicolo, P. (2013) *Achieving Impact in Research*, (Success in Research), Sage Publications Ltd.

Holmberg, K. J. (2015) *Altmetrics for Information Professionals: past, present and future*, Chandos Publishing.

Peltier-Davis, C. A. (2012) *The Cybrarian's Web: an A–Z guide to 101 free Web 2.0 tools and other resources*, Facet Publishing.

Pryor, G. (ed.) (2012) *Managing Research Data*, Facet Publishing.

Roemer, R. C. and Borchardt, R. (2015) *Meaningful Metrics: a 21st century librarian's guide to bibliometrics, almetrics, and research impact*, ALA Editions.

Shorley, D. and Jubb, M. (eds) (2013) *The Future of Scholarly Communication*, Facet Publishing.

Wilsdon, J. et al. (2015) *The Metric Tide: Report of the Independent Review of the Role of Metrics in Research Assessment and Management*, doi:10.13140/RG.2.1.4929.1363.

Index